WHEN Life Happens

AN HONEST LOOK AT THE STUFF THAT
COMES ALONG...

by Sheri Benvenuti

Published by Lifeward Publishing Company, a subsidiary of Lifeward LLC.

Scripture quotations are taken from:

The Message by Eugene H. Peterson, copyright © 1993, 1994, 1995, 1996, 2000, 2001, 2002. Used by permission of NavPress Publishing Group. All rights reserved.

The Holy Bible, New International Version (NIV). Copyright © 1973, 1978, 1984 by International Bible Society. Used by permission of Zondervan. All rights reserved.

Cover design and pagination by Robison Creative Studios | www.robisoncreative.com

ISBN 978-1-933497-23-5

For

Dad and Mom Waugh

whose persistent

encouragement to

"write it all down"

has finally

borne fruit.

TABLE OF CONTENTS

WHEN Life Happens

FOREWORD

I first met Sheri Benvenuti in 1971 when I followed her father as pastor in Newport Beach. As a young single minister, Sheri effectively ministered to a strong group of youth, reaching many from the counter-culture of that era. In the subsequent years she went on to further her preparation for ministry by attaining a doctoral degree and teaching at Vanguard University. The zeal has never departed from her life. She epitomizes what it means to have "knowledge on fire."

In recent years, Sheri has walked through a veil of suffering in the loss of her parents and in battling cancer and disability. She knows what it is like to journey through the valley of the shadow of death.

Out of her life experience she has written this superb inspirational book, ***When Life Happens.*** However, the book is not her biography. Instead, Sheri delves into the experiences of David to show us how to respond when some very traumatic things hit us. Her chapter titles telegraph those hard hits in life—all the way from our dreams dying to a friend betraying us. David knew them all—the ups and many downs that produced his immortal Psalms. Sheri knows something of that as well and complements the lessons of David with her own experiences.

In his fictional biography of Michelangelo, Irving Stone relates the true story of the making of the magnificent David statue. In the Duomo work yards of Florence, Italy, Michelangelo found the Duccio block—a long marble stone with a defect in its center that had caused other sculptors to pass it by for over 50 years out of fear that any art made from it would only crumble. Michelangelo, however, figured out mathematically how to work around the defect, and from that Duccio block came the young 17 feet tall David. This priceless piece of art resulted from a lot of blows with hammer and chisel. In the hands of a lesser artist, David would have never emerged.

It's that way with the real David. Only God saw the potential and could bring it forth. The hard blows David experienced produced the treasury of insight from his own pen. Sheri, likewise, has known what it's like to be "chiseled on" by some pretty tough blows—but, she knows also how God helps us through those seasons when we are screaming, "Life's not fair."

I know this book will be a great encouragement to you and that's why I recommend it!

— *Dr. George O. Wood*
General Superintendent
General Council of the Assemblies of God

INTRODUCTION

On a Monday evening, not all that long ago, I attended the memorial service of a long-standing friend of mine. She had fought a valiant battle against cancer, defying the original prognosis by living nearly five years longer than projected. Even with the sickness and exhaustion she experienced from multiple chemotherapy sessions, Barb remained as vital and fruitful a person as she had ever been. Even though I knew that I would meet her again in the life-to-come, her passing was a significant loss, and I mourned that loss greatly.

On Tuesday night, I was sitting among 15,000 other people at a sold-out Hollywood Bowl event listening to the greatest cellist in all of history, Yo-Yo Ma. My heart soared with the beauty of the music as Ma's fingers danced over the fingerboard of his instrument, his bow slashing from string to string on his 200-year-old Stradivarius cello. My ears and my heart connected as one; it was a miraculous and euphoric experience.

And this, my friends, is just about the way life happens—one night you're mourning, and within twenty-four hours, you're exhilarated. Life seems to go on relatively well for a while, and then you lose your job, or someone dies, or your children rebel, or you make a bad decision. And then, for a while, you have to deal with the fall-out.

This book is about facing the fall-out when life happens.

It's also about understanding that we never face those issues alone.

And because God is always with us, we can actually come out on the other side of the difficulty triumphantly.

I have, of course, turned to scripture to give us the information we need to live life successfully during the times when life happens. I find that one of the most amazing things about the Bible is that there is absolutely no attempt by its writers to conceal the flaws of its major characters. In fact, you almost get the idea that the writers of scripture are more interested in capitalizing on some of their most heinous actions than they are in hiding them. This is one of the most powerful things about the Bible. These are characters that I can actually identify with. They are people who really love God, but from time to time, say the wrong thing, think evil thoughts, and involve themselves in sinful activity, yet are able to experience radical deliverance simply because in the end, they turn back to the God who loves them so much.

David, son of Jesse and probably the most famous of Israel's kings, is one such character in scripture. Historian Abram Leon Sachar says of King David, "He played exquisitely, he fought heroically, he loved titanically. Withal he was a profoundly simple being, cheerful, despondent; selfish, generous; sinning one moment, repenting the next; the most human character of the Bible."

As Sachar suggests, the paradox of David's life really is stunning. On the one hand, we find that hiding somewhere deep in David's character is a seducer and a murderer as he takes the lovely Bathsheba to his royal bed and then contrives to kill her husband, Uriah, after Bathsheba is found to be pregnant with David's child.

On the other hand, David is equally portrayed as, "a man after God's own heart" (1 Samuel 13:4), a man who was God's choice to reign on earth. Even in death, David is seen as the precursor to and the direct ancestor of the Messiah who was to come and redeem humankind: "And there shall come forth a shoot out of the stock of Jesse, and a twig shall grow forth out of his roots," says the prophet Isaiah (Isaiah 11:1).

How do we explain the amazing paradox' of David's life? Sachar observes that in the end, David has a unique ability to comply with God's *will*, even while he finds it difficult to be obedient to God's *law* at times. The thing that saves David in the midst of this paradox is that he knows how to repent and knows well the God who is always willing to forgive him.

Boy, can we ever identify with David! Just like David, we can love God with all of our hearts, but know deep in our souls that we have the tremendous ability to really blow it.

Equally difficult, is the utterly exhausting effort of trying to work through issues that arise as a result of just living life.

The truth is, the majority of experiences in David's life had little to do with overtly sinful acts. Life simply happened to David in the same way life happens to us. David knew what it meant to be rejected by friends and family; he understood sheer terror; he experienced hunger and thirst and a lack of the most basic comforts of life; he even knew the sorrow of raising rebellious children. The amazing thing to me is that David actually seemed to be able, in the end, to work through all of this "stuff of life" successfully!

So, in just living life, David has given all of us, about 3,000 years later, the great benefit of his experiences.

The wonderful thing about studying David's life experiences is that not only do we have entire books of the Bible written about him, we also have a massive amount of stuff written by David, most of which can be found in the Book of Psalms. When we put this information together, we get a kind of two-pronged study approach: the stories in the Old Testament that describe David's life experiences (the stuff written about him) and David's own inward responses to those life circumstances (the stuff written by him).

While we can't identify all of David's Psalms with specific situations in his life, many of the Psalms written by David actually include a description of the circumstances during which David wrote that particular Psalm. When I open my Bible to Psalm 51, for example, this is exactly how it is printed:

Psalm 51

For the director of music. A psalm of David. When the prophet Nathan came to him after David had committed adultery with Bathsheba.

Have mercy on me, O God, according to your unfailing love; according to your great compassion blot out my transgressions.

Wash away all my iniquity and cleanse me from my sin.

As you can see from the sub-title, David wrote Psalm 51 "when the prophet Nathan came to him after David had committed adultery with Bathsheba." The particular circumstance of David's life that this Psalm describes is written **about** David in 2 Samuel 11 and 12. This story gives us all of the gory details of David's act of adultery with Bathsheba, the murder of Uriah, Bathsheba's husband, and the Prophet Nathan's public rebuke of David's actions. We even have David's response to Nathan: "I have sinned against the Lord" (2 Samuel 12:13).

But thanks to Psalm 51, we also have David's own writing about this event in his life. This gives us a real "insiders" view of how David felt, what he was thinking, and even how he was attempting to resolve the difficulties of this life circumstance.

Look at the prose David uses in this Psalm. "Have mercy on me, O God...Wash away all my iniquity and cleanse me from my sin." Can't you just picture David on his face before God, speaking to God from the depths of his own heart? The truth is, without Psalm 51, we wouldn't really have the full story of how David actually dealt with the adultery and murder; we need David's own words to fill in all the blanks. So, while in 2 Samuel 12:13 we find David's **admission** of guilt, Psalm 51 explores that way in which he actually **works through** his guilt.

Just using the few beginning verses of the Psalm as a guide, what can we learn about David's response to his great sins? Did David attempt to just live with the guilt of his wrongdoing? Did he try to shove it under the rug? Did David come up with justification for his actions: "I'm the King, and I can do what I want?" Absolutely not! Instead, David took his guilt to

God and appealed to His mercy, asking God to "wash away" all of his iniquity and to "cleanse" him from sin. And, this, my friend, is exactly what we should do with our guilt. We don't live with it, we don't hide it, we don't justify it. Rather, just like David, we should run to God and ask for forgiveness for the actions that caused the guilt in the first place.

This is the methodology I have used throughout this book. First, we'll look at some of the most poignant life circumstances written **about** David's life. Then, we'll look at the comparative Psalm written **by** David during those circumstances. The result of this study should give us new insight into how we can begin to deal with our own issues and the fall-out that inevitably occurs when life happens to us.

I pray that as you work your way through these pages, God will bring greater understanding to you about His amazing goodness, and His incomparable ability to bring wholeness into your life.

Chapter 1

WHEN A LEADER FAILS

1 Samuel 15 & Psalm 52

I have always said that if I ever found the perfect church, the moment I stepped inside the front door, it wouldn't be perfect any longer.

The truth is, humanity is tremendously broken. And while the act of receiving Christ as Savior brings amazing spiritual transformation to individuals, salvation really is ground zero for the kind of repair that God wants to do in our lives. The reality is that church buildings are filled with folks who are in different stages of growth toward wholeness. As a result, it's imperative that we're quick to love and forgive, and slow to hurt and anger—Christians we may be, but perfect we are not.

I'll confess to you, though, that I have been absolutely stunned with the level of failure among church leaders we've heard about in recent years. One leader's failure in particular caught my attention because of the far-reaching ramifications of his actions.

Ted Haggard was born in Indiana in 1956 to a veterinarian father practicing in Yorktown. He wasn't raised in church, but at age 16 accepted Christ as Savior after hearing a sermon preached by evangelical leader, Rev. Bill Bright.

After graduating from Oral Roberts University in 1978, Ted Haggard spent five years on the ministry staff at Bethany Baptist Church in Baker, Louisiana. Haggard tells the story that while on a camping trip near Colorado Springs, Colorado, he felt God urging him to remain in the area. In 1985, he founded his New Life Church in the basement of a Colorado Springs home.

It is said that Haggard, an avowed Charismatic, bought oil in bulk for anointing and literally turned cartwheels as part of his charismatic style. Attendance outgrew his basement within weeks, forcing moves into progressively larger rented spaces, including strip malls and other non-traditional church locations. The church established its present campus location in the early 1990s and developed their property by adding new buildings and adding on to existing buildings. Twenty years after its founding, New Life Church had 14,000 members and owned a huge sanctuary that seated 8,000 at a time.

He was not only tremendously successful as a pastor, Haggard was also active outside his church. He was elected President of the National

Association of Evangelicals (NAE) in 2003. The NAE was founded just after World War II, in an effort to foster cross-denominational support among Protestant congregations instead of emphasis on public disputes over the different doctrines of various denominations. The NAE now includes some 43,000 churches with about 30 million members in 51 denominations. Because of its huge constituency (second only to the Catholic Church), the NAE has become a very visible entity within American social and political life, offering anyone who leads the organization a great deal of power.

This power not only extends to the membership of the NAE itself, but also has become a target for many conservative politicians who salivate at the thought of 30 million possible votes. Because of Haggard's position as president of the organization, it wasn't long before he began to hob-knob with many of the rich and powerful. While the NAE never offers official backing for any political candidates, Haggard actually did enjoy quite a bit of political clout. Author Jeff Sharlet reported in *Harper's* that Haggard "talks to... [President] Bush or his advisers every Monday" and stated at that time that "no pastor in America holds more sway over the political direction of evangelicalism (Sharlet, 2005). In 2005, *The Wall Street Journal* reported that Haggard had joked that the only disagreement between him and the leader of the Western world is automotive: Mr. Bush drives a Ford pickup, whereas he prefers a Chevy (Wooldridge, 2005).

This is a man who had everything going for him. He pastored a huge church, headed the NAE, was often invited to the White House, was married to a beautiful wife, had five children, and authored three books. Haggard had been called the second-most powerful evangelical leader in

America, just slightly behind evangelical psychologist, James Dobson and was listed by *Time* magazine as one of the top 25 most influential evangelicals in America (*TIME* Names the 15 Most Influential Evangelicals in America, 2005).

In November 2006, however, Pastor Ted Haggard resigned from his leadership of the National Association of Evangelicals, and stepped down from the pulpit of his 14,000-member New Life Church amid allegations that he had regularly purchased methamphetamines and paid for regular trysts with a gay prostitute.

Sadly, Haggard joined a list of other notorious Christian leaders. Preacher Jim Bakker, a ferocious and proud man in the pulpit, fell from grace because of sex scandals and fraud even spending time in jail for his crimes. Tele-evangelist Jimmy Swaggart, who helped expose Bakker, calling him "a cancer in the body of Christ," was at the same time meeting with prostitutes in local motel rooms. Not only is this kind of behavior part of the recent history of the Evangelical Church, but it extends to other denominations as well. The sexual problems of the Catholic clergy are, to me, indescribable in their sordidness, with the Catholic Church paying out millions of dollars to victims of sexual abuse.

While these high-profile cases of leadership failure are terrible in their own right, what is really horrible is that misconduct by leaders in local churches has reached almost epidemic proportions. Many top leaders of evangelical denominations admit that responding to leadership misconduct among their pastors, evangelists and missionaries, takes up much of their time.

How is it that leaders in our churches, many of whom have had a relationship with the Lord for all of their lives, can commit such heinous sins? We're talking the Church, after all! Shouldn't the Church actually be a sanctuary where God's people feel safe from any misuse of power by, or abuse from their leaders?

Unfortunately, this kind of behavior coming from leaders is certainly not a new thing. Scripture, in fact, is very forthright when it comes to talking about leadership failure.

Throughout the early part of the Old Testament, God Himself acted as King of Israel, with individuals chosen by God to be priests, prophets and judges who would carry out the will of the King among His people. There came a time, however, when the prophet Samuel was old and decided to take it upon himself to appoint his sons as judges over Israel. The elders of Israel were not happy about this arrangement and for good reason. Both of Samuel's sons, Joel and Abijah, "did not walk in [Samuel's] ways. They turned aside after dishonest gain and accepted bribes and perverted justice" (1 Samuel 8:2-3). But the elder's solution to the problem was tantamount to rejecting God as their king. They said to Samuel, "Appoint a king to lead us, such as all the other nations have." God's response to the elder's desire was to create a list of demands a human king would make upon the people, demands that God Himself would never make upon them:

- He will take your sons and make them serve with his chariots and horses, and they will run in front of his chariots.
- Some he will assign to be commanders of thousands and commanders of fifties, and others to plow his ground and reap his harvest, and still others to make weapons of war and equipment for his chariots.
- He will take your daughters to be perfumers and cooks and bakers.
- He will take the best of your fields and vineyards and olive groves and give them to his attendants.
- He will take a tenth of your grain and of your vintage and give it to his officials and attendants. Your menservants and maidservants and the best of your cattle and donkeys he will take for his own use.
- He will take a tenth of your flocks, and you yourselves will become his slaves.
- When that day comes, you will cry out for relief from the king you have chosen, and the LORD will not answer you in that day.

You'd think this kind of dire warning would have given the elders a clue. But the people refused to listen to Samuel. "No!" they insisted. "We want a king over us. Then we will be like all the other nations, with a king to lead us and to go out before us and fight our battles." When Samuel heard all that the people said, he went before the Lord and repeated everything. The LORD answered, "Listen to them and give them a king."

So, God chose "an impressive young man without equal among the Israelites—a head taller than any of the others" (1 Samuel 9:2) to become King over his people. His name was Saul.

God did everything to prepare Saul to become King: Samuel poured a flask of oil over his head saying, "Has not the Lord anointed you leader over his inheritance?" In addition, "God changed Saul's heart," and "came upon him in power" (1 Samuel 10:1, 6).

Saul was 30 years old when he became king, and reigned over Israel for 42 years. Saul had everything going for him: he led successful campaigns against Israel's arch-enemy, the Philistines, enjoyed a great deal of power among his own people, and earned a fearful reputation with the other nations around him. Saul even had a great son named Jonathan, groomed to be heir to the throne. About twenty-five years into his reign, however, something began to happen to Saul. He began to take authority that was not his to take. He started to take matters into his own hands, even so far as breaking the commandments of God. The story of Saul's leadership failure begins with one of the great stories in the Old Testament involving a Semitic people called the Amalekites.

The first important thing to know about the Amalekites is that they were not nice people. They were an incredibly war-like tribe, attacking any people they came across in their nomadic existence. Living somewhere in the Negev and Sinai, the Amalekites followed and harassed the Israelites from the moment God miraculously led them out of slavery in Egypt and through the Red Sea. Because Israel had no standing army and no weapons to speak of during this time, they became easy pickings for the evil Amalekites.

The second thing to know about the Amalekites is that they fought dirty. They covertly followed the Israelites, biding their time until the sun was about to go down and the Israelites had gotten weary and worn out from their journey across the desert. Then they would strike, slaughtering all of the people lagging behind who were too tired, too young, or too old to keep up. Even beyond these dirty tactics, the Amalekites had no fear of Israel's God—a major mistake when you're trying to subdue God's people.

Israel finally responded to the Amalekite attacks and went to war against them in a place called Rephidim, a city about 25 miles northwest of Mt. Sinai. It is here that a great story takes place in which the Israelite's victory in the war depended upon their leader, Moses, keeping his hands raised. So, with the help of one man on each side of Moses, each holding up one hand, Israel won the day; truly a miraculous event since this was the first fighting these ex-slaves had ever done. In spite of winning the battle, however, God was not pleased that Israel had to fight them. In fact, after the battle was over, God commanded Moses to write down these words so that the people of Israel would always remember them: "I will completely blot out the memory of [the Amalekites] from under heaven," God said (Exodus 17:14).

God never forgot what he had told Moses and the people. Several years later, as Israel was approaching the land that God had promised them, God once again reminded Israel of his view of the Amalekites:

> *When the Lord your God gives you rest from all the enemies around you in the land he is giving you to possess as an inheritance, you shall blot out the memory of Amalek from under heaven. Do not forget!* (Deuteronomy 25:19)

Several hundred years later, after Saul had become King of Israel, it was time for God to bring judgment upon the Amalekites. And a harsh judgment it was! God's prophet, Samuel, said to Saul one day: "O King, I've heard from the Lord Almighty and this is what he says: 'I will punish the Amalekites for what they did to Israel when they waylaid them as they came up from Egypt.' Now go attack the Amalekites and totally destroy everything that belongs to them. Do nothing to spare them; put to death men and women, children and infants, cattle and sheep, camels and donkeys" (ref. 1 Samuel 15:1-4).

While this sounds like an incredibly harsh thing to do, the God of Justice was determined to do to the Amalekites exactly what they had done to Israel: kill the old, the women, the children—everyone unable to keep up.

So, King Saul went to war, with the result that the Amalekites were totally routed. However, instead of following the instructions of the Lord, he left Agag, King of the Amalekites alive, and Israel's army took all of the Amalekite's herds as booty. It wasn't enough that King Saul flagrantly disobeyed God's command to kill everyone and everything; in addition, he set up a monument in his own honor in a town nearby the battleground in order to perpetually remind Israel of what a great king he was.

How did God respond to Saul's actions? God sent Samuel to talk to Saul yet one more time, only this time, the message was not good news. Samuel said to Saul, "Although you were once small in your own eyes, didn't God make you the king of all the tribes of Israel? The Lord anointed you king over Israel and then he sent you on a mission commanding you to,

'Go and completely destroy those wicked people, the Amalekites; make war on them until you have wiped them out.' "Why didn't you obey the Lord," Samuel asked. "Why did you pounce on the plunder and do evil in the eyes of the Lord? There are always ramifications for disobeying God's commands, O King. And this is yours: Because you have rejected the word of the Lord, he has rejected you as King. The Lord has torn the kingdom of Israel from you today and has given it to one of your neighbors—to one better than you" (ref. 1 Samuel 15:17-19).

Why do leaders fail? This story demonstrates two huge reasons— **disobedience to God** and **unbridled arrogance**. If you look at King Saul's 42- year reign over Israel, you will discover these two elements continually plaguing his leadership; he was so arrogant that not only did he not listen to God, but actually seemed to feel that he knew better than God.

It is vital to note that Saul remained King of Israel for several more years after the battle with the Amalekites. So, what is this about "tearing the Kingdom of Israel" from Saul? Well, because of Saul's flagrant disobedience, he ruled Israel without God ever speaking to him again. Scripture says that until the day Samuel died, he did not go to see Saul again, though Samuel mourned for him. And the Lord was actually grieved that he had made Saul king over Israel.

Can you imagine ruling an entire nation without ever hearing God's voice? Praying and never hearing an answer? Needing supernatural direction for decisions you have to make and never receiving any help? Simply said, if you consistently fail to listen to God and disobey Him, you run the risk that He will just stop talking to you and begin to talk to someone else. In King Saul's case, the "someone else" was a teen-aged shepherd boy by the name of David.

What made things even worse for King Saul was that the King-in-waiting David was living in his own household where he could see first-hand God's hand upon him. This was so obvious that scripture says, "Saul was afraid of David, because the Lord was with David but had left Saul" (1 Samuel 18:12). Saul hated David because of it. In fact, King Saul hated David so much that he tried to kill him twice in one day. Even when David left Saul's household, running for his life, the king began to hunt him down like an animal.

In his continued flight from King Saul, David ended up one day in the city of Nob where a large contingent of priests lived. Not a bad place to go if you're looking for somewhere safe! David, however, did not receive a cordial welcome from the head priest, Ahimelech. In fact, "Ahimelech trembled when he met David," and as it turns out, Ahimelech had a right to tremble!

When King Saul found out that David had run to Nob to hide, he sent for Priest Ahimelech and asked him, "Why have you conspired against me by giving David bread and a sword and inquiring of God for him?"

Ahimelech answered him by saying, "Listen! David is your son-in-law, the captain of your bodyguard and highly respected by everyone. Why shouldn't I give him bread and a sword and inquire of the Lord on his behalf?"

Saul's response? "Kill them, kill them all!"

The king's men, however, were too afraid to kill the priests of the Lord. So, King Saul turned to one of his mercenaries, Doeg the Edomite, and commanded him to do the dirty work. Doeg, who had no qualms about killing Israelite priests, murdered not only Ahimelech, but also an additional 85 priests. And Doeg didn't stop there. He also killed all the men, all the women, all the children, the cattle, donkeys and sheep living in Nod.

How heinous was this? What King Saul refused to do to Israel's archenemy, the Amalekites, he did to his own people! How far God's chosen leader had fallen!

David wrote about Saul after the horrible slaughter of innocents occurred in Nob. You'll find his poem in Psalm 52:

> *Why do you boast of evil, you mighty man? Why do you boast all day long, you who are a disgrace in the eyes of God? Your tongue plots destruction; it is like a sharpened razor, you who practice deceit. You love evil rather than good, falsehood rather than speaking the truth.*
>
> *You love every harmful word, O you deceitful tongue! Surely God will bring you down to everlasting ruin. He will snatch you up and tear you from your tent; he will uproot you from the land of the living.*
>
> *The righteous will see and fear; they will laugh at him, saying, "Here now is the man who did not make God his stronghold but trusted in his great wealth and grew strong by destroying others! (vv.1-7)*

I once worked for a Saul. At the beginning of his tenure as the leader of our non-profit organization, it was clear that he was God's choice. He led with the massive support of those who were in the organization, and because God's hand was upon him, he even gained great favor with the community at large. But as the months passed, I watched him begin to make decisions based more on marketing strategy than on God's direction; to hire mere "yes-men" and make them his confidants rather than listening to the godly people the Lord set around him. And even worse, he actually began to believe his own press; he believed that the growth and success of the organization had only to do with his great leadership ability, rather than the blessing of God on his life.

I can mark the day that God stopped talking to him. It was the day he publicly proclaimed to several of us, "I'm the leader; I can do what I want."

Just like King Saul, now relegated to leading without the voice of God guiding him, this leader did exactly what he wanted to do, making decisions that went from bad to worse; some of those decisions were fearfully close to being illegal. Within two years he was forced by the governing board to resign, leaving the organization millions of dollars in debt with people wondering how in the world the organization could have spiraled downward in such a short time.

While this leader certainly did not kill off everything breathing in the city of Nob as King Saul had commanded Doeg to do, the hurt that the people employed in the organization went through during this time was agonizing. Individuals who had worked for this organization for decades were laid off; programs were cut. When some of the more questionable business practices were brought to light and the story was picked up by the local newspaper, dozens of faithful Christian employees and friends of the organization were humiliated and embarrassed that such things could have gone on in a Christian organization.

You see, it isn't just the failure of the leader that is so appalling. It is the resultant carnage that everyone close to him has to deal with that is so horrifying. Of his own situation, Ted Haggard said, "My wife—all my sin and shame fell on her. People treated her as if she had fallen. And my children—they all went through carrying my shame." When a leader fails, it's not just the sorrow, the anger and the sense of betrayal everyone feels about him or her, it's also about the "slaughter" of the innocents that occurs as a result of leadership failure. It's the 44 people who were laid off at New Life Church due to falling church income four months after Haggard's resignation. It's about the hundreds of kids in Central America who lost funding for their education because a fallen tele-evangelist couldn't meet his missions budget after he failed. It's about the hundreds who died and the thousands of family members who grieved when Jim Jones fed cyanide to his followers in the jungles of Guyana.

Why is it that God allows innocent people to suffer because of the mistakes of others? Where is God in the situation, and how do we cope with all of this?

While David did not give us a full understanding into the "why" questions we always seem to ask at times like these, he did give us an insight into what our stance and response should be in these situations. David ended Psalm 52 in this way:

> *But I am like an olive tree flourishing in the house of God;*
> *I trust in God's unfailing love forever and ever.*
> *I will praise you forever for what you have done; in your name*
> *I will hope, for your name is good.*
> *I will praise you in the presence of your saints* (vv.8-9).

The first thing to notice about these verses is that where God promises in the first part of the Psalm to uproot the Saul-like leader "from the land of the living," the righteous person standing by, conversely, is like an olive tree "flourishing in the house of God."

David chose to use an interesting illustration to describe the righteous person because of the nature of the tree itself. Olive trees are incredibly sturdy trees; their roots go deep. They can survive drought, survive frost and can live for literally thousands of years. Further, olive oil was the preferred fat used in cooking because olive oil could be kept for a long time without going bad. The oil was also used to make soap to cleanse and ointments to heal. And notice where the tree is planted—it is planted "in the house of God."

David's message to us when a leader fails? While "life happens" all around us, and we feel threatened by hurtful circumstances, the righteous person finds his or her roots deep in the soil of the presence of God. And not only do the righteous survive leadership failure, but the soil found in the house of the Lord is so lush that our fruitfulness during these times can actually provide oil for cleansing and ointment for healing. Out of this can come the assistance so needed for those who have been hurt most. So, rather than being just one more casualty of failed leadership, the righteous person realizes who he or she is, and in doing so, responds to the circumstance in a positive way.

We also learn other vital lessons from this scriptural passage that help us negotiate life during times of leadership failure. David declares in the last three stanzas of Psalm 52, "I will trust," "I will praise," and "I will hope."

David's first declaration, "I will trust," is a difficult thing for anyone to do. It's difficult because trust is always grounded in relationship—we've learned to trust someone because that person has proven him or herself trustworthy over a period of time. Trust is especially difficult when that trust has been violated by a sinful leader in whom we once placed our confidence. But then again, maybe that's just the problem: we trusted in the sinful leader. David says, "I will trust **in God's** unfailing love." It is a hard lesson that we seem to need to learn over and over again—humans are fallible. And, while we can trust our leaders to a degree, it is only in God that we can fully trust. In fact, the Hebrew word for "trust" used here also carries the idea of feeling safe.

The point is that God can always be trusted because He is entirely trustworthy; He is unfailing. Not only is it God's character to be trustworthy, but David also said that He loves us with an unfailing love. God's love for us is never based on what we do or don't do, but rather is based on His own loving character; God is love and that fact never changes. Interestingly, one translation of verse 8 is, "*I trust in God's loyal-love, (which lasts) forever and ever.*" God loves me, and I can trust him!

On the other hand, the second declaration, "I will praise," is not all that difficult to do, especially when things are going great. We all know a great many songs we sing with great conviction about how wonderful God is. However, it is not an easy task to praise God when people's hearts are breaking. Praise in these kinds of situations always becomes an act of trust. That is to say, if I really trust God to be working in the circumstance, I will praise Him just as if He has already intervened. Praise is never about me, never about my situation; praise is always about God. In fact, the word for "praise" that David used here literally means "to throw," or "to cast." It is a word that was used to describe the act of shooting an arrow at a target. Praise is my arrow, and God is my target. I praise Him because no matter what the outcome of this situation will be, I can trust God to end things well.

Last, David declared that he will hope in God's name because God's name is good. The word used for "hope" in this passage is *yawdah*. This word actually has a double meaning. It means "to look for" and, in addition, "to wait for." Hope then, means to wait with great anticipation. And this hope, according to David, is based on God's "name," or better understood, upon God's reputation. God has a great **reputation** for doing things well, even though we may not understand His technique. But then, that's part of trusting God as well.

There is an old hymn, written one Sunday in 1863 that so well describes the kind of trust, faith and hope we should have in God. As the story goes, a man by the name of Edward Mote made his way to his country church one morning. He had written down a few verses of a song that he had started composing some days before and was pondering how he should continue the lyrics. Upon arriving at church, he was met by Mr. King, a friend whose wife was deathly ill; Mote was asked if he could visit her. Later in the afternoon, Mote entered the King house to find Mrs. King near death. Mote read her a few passages of scripture, prayed, and then asked if it would be alright if he sang the four verses of the song he was writing. Mrs. King found so much strength in those few verses that she asked Mote to leave a copy of them with her so she could refer to them in the difficult days ahead. Mote was so moved at the influence the verses had on Mrs. King, that when he returned home, he was able to finish the entire song. The words to the now very familiar hymn are these:

> My hope is built on nothing less
> Than Jesus' blood and righteousness.
> I dare not trust the sweetest frame,
> But wholly trust in Jesus' Name.
>
> *Refrain:*
>
> *On Christ the solid Rock I stand,*
> *All other ground is sinking sand;*
> *All other ground is sinking sand.*
>
> When darkness seems to hide His face,
> I rest on His unchanging grace.
> In every high and stormy gale,
> My anchor holds within the veil.
>
> *Refrain*

His oath, His covenant, His blood,
Support me in the whelming flood.
When all around my soul gives way,
He then is all my Hope and Stay.

Refrain

When He shall come with trumpet sound,
Oh may I then in Him be found.
Dressed in His righteousness alone,
Faultless to stand before the throne.

Oh, yes. While David put his hope and trust in God, it's important to remember the end of this story. It's not a happy ending for two reasons: first, because the end of King Saul's reign over Israel was also the end of his life. And, second, the end of King Saul's life was not an easy end.

In the very last chapter of 1 Samuel, the author tells us that the Philistines fought against Israel yet one more time, but this time Israel found itself on the losing side—the Philistines totally routed Israel's army. All of Israel's soldiers fled, leaving King Saul and his sons on Mount Gilboa, exposed to the enemy. Clearly seeing Saul without any protection, the Philistines pressed their advantage, killed Saul's sons Jonathan, Abinadab and Malki-Shua, and critically wounded Saul himself. When Saul's armor-bearer refused to give Saul a quick end to his life, Saul fell on his own sword and died. That day, just as God had declared, the Kingdom of Israel was torn from Saul.

What a waste! This horrible circumstance could have been avoided altogether had King Saul been the kind of leader who listened to and obeyed God.

I don't know why it is that God doesn't just supernaturally intervene when leaders fail, or why He allows innocent people to suffer the fall-out. I do know, however, that in the midst of the sorrow and hurt and anger, God's righteous ones continue to dig their roots deep in the soil of God's unfailing love and wait with great hope and anticipation for His will to be done.

So, how does this play out in one's life? What exactly does digging your roots deep in the soil look like?

Recently, Ted Haggard and his wife, Gayle, appeared on the *Oprah Winfrey Show* (Haggard, 2010). The interview was done mainly for the purpose of highlighting Gayle's new book, *Why I Stayed: The Choices I Made in my Darkest Hour.*

It really surprised me to learn that Gayle, Ted's wife of 30 years, heard about the accusations against her husband the same way everyone else did—during the interview Mike Jones, Haggard's accuser, gave on the radio in November 2006. After hearing the broadcast, Gayle said she found the accusations so absurd that she actually laughed when she heard what Jones was accusing her husband of doing. The use of drugs rang especially false to Gayle. "I thought, [Mike] obviously does not know my husband," Gayle said, "because my husband didn't drink alcohol, didn't smoke cigarettes. Not even in high school did he tamper with any kind of drugs," she said.

After the radio interview aired, Gayle and Ted went to their attorney's office to deal with how they were going to handle this horrible slander; at least that's what Gayle thought. But when they reached the office, the attorney told Gayle that she and Ted needed to talk privately before he consulted with them. When the attorney left the office and shut the door, Ted told her the unthinkable. "He said, 'Gayle, part of this is true.' And the first words out of my mouth," Gayle said, "were: 'Who are you?'"

In the days that followed, Ted came clean with Gayle about his sexual immorality and drug use. "I can't think of anything that would have been a greater shock to me, and, literally, I felt as though the rug had been pulled out from under me," Gayle said.

Yet, she stayed by her husband's side. "I was going to stay with Ted because, first of all, I love him deeply, and I knew that we had a very real relationship," she said. "I choose to forgive him, and I choose to love him. I made the decision. Then I had to work it out. And that was the painful process for me."

As you can imagine, the scandal also deeply affected their five children. Marcus and Christy, the two oldest Haggard children, recalled hearing the news about their Dad in a family meeting. While they were aware of the accusations of their father's activities through the media, Marcus said hearing his father's admission of the truth was altogether different. "It was a sad meeting, but the decisiveness—it was so humbling," he says. "There was an immediate relief that I think we felt as kids—mixed with anger, frustration."

Christy also admitted that their family meeting was a revelation. "I never had a dad I felt I could really relate to," she said. "And suddenly to see this vulnerable, honest man in front of me opened an opportunity for me to really know who my father really was for the first time."

Marcus said the family chose not dwell on the details of their dad's sexuality. Instead, they focused on keeping the family together. "We knew that this kind of thing had the potential to rip our family apart. ... We committed to working through the anger, the frustration, the sadness, the yelling and stomping out, the fights that we would have to go through," he said. "We committed to go through that process so that we could be committed to each other" (Oprah.com, 2009).

Gayle says of this time in, *Why I Stayed:*

Though I was shocked, heartbroken, and afraid, I felt as though I had spent my entire life training for that moment. I thought about my faith in God and my belief in the Bible. I considered my convictions about marriage and family, friendship, and the body of Christ; concepts I had taught to the women of our church.

I realized that everything I believed was being tested. Now I had to determine whether I had the strength to pass the test. Everything I valued was at stake; my marriage, my children, my church, and my understanding of God.

In those quiet moments, I decided to rise to the challenge. I was going to demonstrate my love by fighting for the dignity and honor of everyone and everything I held dear.

I had no idea how the battle would take shape; I had no idea how the opposition would present itself; but that night I settled the question within my own mind: My faith and the people I loved were worth fighting for. So fight I would, no matter how difficult the battle (Haggard, 2010).

Whether we do or do not agree with Gayle's decision to stay with her husband, it seems that in doing so, Gayle has really learned what David was talking about. Instead of being a casualty of her husband's actions, she rather chose to dig her roots deep in the soil of God's unfailing love. Instead of living in hurt and pain, Gayle has chosen to wait with great hope and anticipation for God's final will to be done.

I am telling you. God has the ability to bring great healing and new hope to the person who has been bruised by a fallen leader. Please don't live your life as a victim, locked into hurt and hopelessness. Rather, dig your roots deep into your relationship with the God who has the ability to restore you and to bring a sense of hopefulness back into your life. Be like David, who declared during one of the most hurtful and disappointing times in his life, "I **will** trust God, I **will** praise God, and I **will** hope in God."

Works Cited

Haggard, G. (2010, January 18). Oprah Winfrey Show. (O. Winfrey, Interviewer)

Haggard, G. (2010). *Why I Stayed: The Choices I Made in my Darkest Hour.* Carol Stream, IL: Tyndale House.

Oprah.com. (2009, June 30). Retrieved January 30, 2010, from Oprah Winfrey Show: www.oprah.com/oprahshow/Ted-Haggard-Talks

Sharlet, J. (2005, May). Soldiers of Christ: 1. Inside America's Most Powerful Megachurch. *Harper's* , p. 42.

TIME Names the 15 Most Influential Evangelicals in America. (2005, January 30). *Time* .

Wooldridge, J. M. (2005, June 21). Cheer Up, Conservatives! *Wall Street Journal* .

WHEN A DREAM DIES

1 Samuel 19 – Psalm 59

I worked with a great senior pastor. I filled the role of Youth Pastor for several years then became his Associate Pastor. What a mentor! Pastor would sit in my office, or I in his, and just talk ministry, formulating better ways to reach people's needs, and many times, to simply pray.

I was in my early thirties when Pastor began to niggle at me about taking some classes at the local Christian college. Honestly, I thought it would be a waste of my time. After all, I was a preacher's kid, had been in ministry for about fourteen years up to that point, and thought I had a pretty thorough knowledge of scripture. But Pastor was so insistent that I finally gave in. I figured if he wanted to give me the time off during the day to attend class, I'd just take advantage of it.

So, I enrolled in two classes—a total of five units: New Testament Survey and Introduction to Theology. Both, I thought, had "A" written all over them.

The first day I walked into NT Survey, a kid from the youth group in our church was sitting in the front row. "Hey, Sheri!" he said. "Are you going to teach this class?"

OK, how embarrassing is this? "No," I said. "I'm here to learn just like you." Oh, brother.

When the actual professor did walk in, he greeted us, prayed, and then asked us to take out a piece of paper and put our name on it—we were about to have the first pop quiz of the semester. I thought no problem... this was in the bag.

"First question," he said. "Who was Antiochus Epiphanes?" Wait a minute. Antiochus who? I frantically searched my mind for any time I had ever seen that name in the New Testament. Was he in the lineage of Jesus? One of Paul's evangelist buddies?

"Question two," the professor intoned. "What was Mark's nickname?" Are you kidding me? Mark had a nickname?

"Question three. In which dialect of Greek was the New Testament written?" I can't tell you how tempted I was just to write, "It's all Greek to me" on that line.

Needless to say, I failed miserably at the first pop quiz of the semester, but learned the most invaluable lesson of my life up to that point—I didn't know all that much about scripture, or indeed, most things at all. In my Introduction to Theology class, I began learning about a God I had never heard of before—the transcendent God who lives outside of space and time while at the same time the immanent God whose presence invades every area of my life. I was hooked.

The next semester I took 15 units, then 21 units the semester following. Education began to affect me on so many levels that I felt as if I was becoming a new person.

On the first day of class of my junior year at the College, I stood in Convocation chapel with the rest of the student body, giving honor to the faculty as they marched down the aisle, dressed in their regalia, to find their seats in the front of the auditorium. My heart was struck at that moment with an amazing amount of appreciation for all of those teacher/mentors who had helped transform my life. Then, the thought suddenly hit me— this is what I wanted to do. I wanted to have as much influence on young lives as these professors had on mine. In a moment, the entire thrust of my life was changed. In my mid-thirties, God had given me a brand new dream. Wow.

You need a lot of education to teach at a college level, and I began to feel the pressure of time since I was many years behind the average college graduate. I finished my undergraduate work in three and one-half years and enrolled in the Master's program in Biblical Studies at the College. In the fall of my last year in that program, I began to apply to Ph.D. programs. Having become somewhat of a golden-haired girl at the College, I had received several great letters of recommendation from the faculty, my G.P.A. was near perfect, and I had done well on the Graduate Record Examinations. Needless to say, I felt pretty confident that I would be accepted somewhere.

When I mentioned the name of the University of my choice to the Director of my Master's program, he told me that he had connections to a small Christian College in the area and thought he could secure me an adjunct teaching position in their Religion Department while I was attending the University. He made a few calls, and sure enough, they expressed joy at the possibility of my coming to teach.

While my pastor knew what I was thinking, I hadn't shared any of my plans with the congregation since my plans would, of course, require my resignation from my position at the church. But a man approached me one Sunday morning and told me that he had a dream the night before that he was helping me move to another location. "Are you planning to move away?" he asked.

So this was the confidence I had in my heart for my future: a God-given dream, a job waiting for me, and a random guy who had a dream that I was moving. What more did I need to let me know that I was on the right track? Granted, I did need my letter of acceptance into the Ph.D. program at the University, but with everything falling in place so beautifully, I felt the letter was imminent.

A few weeks later, I received THE letter. I ripped it open immediately. It said, "Dear Sheri: We are sorry to inform you..." What a minute! **"Sorry to inform me?"** This had to be a mistake! They must have gotten confused. Someone had gotten my letter of acceptance, and I'd gotten their rejection letter.

The next morning, I phoned the man who had signed the letter – the Dean of the School of Religion at the University. When I told him who I was, he replied, "Oh. You got your letter." I could tell by the tone of his voice that there was no mistake after all. My heart sunk to my toes. I asked why I hadn't been accepted. I got a lot of, "ums," and "uhs," but no concrete reasons. So I tried to change his mind. I was smart; I was qualified; I was motivated; I would make the University proud. But he wouldn't budge. "These are committee decisions, you know." I wanted to scream into the phone, "How dare you stand in the way of God's plan for my life! I have a God-given dream. I even have a job! What's wrong with you?!" Instead, I just said, "Good-bye," and hung up the phone. I was crushed. My dream was dead. What now?

Have you ever had a dream and seen it dashed to pieces? The trouble with dreams is that we invest so much of ourselves in them. We pour our time, money, energy into them; sometimes dreams are the focal point of our lives and the great hope for our future. When dreams die, it feels like there's nothing left.

David knew what letting a dream die was all about. In the beginning of his life, he really had no hope for a dream. He was the last of eight sons in his family – no hope for any inheritance or even a rich or beautiful wife. He was a young shepherd boy living in Bethlehem and would probably always be a shepherd. The truth is, if you never have a dream in the first place, personal devastation is not quite so possible. So, there's David, sitting on a hill watching his sheep, strumming his harp, making up songs of praise to the God he loved so much. But in the middle of this quite idyllic life, David receives a God-dream. This is how the story begins:

In 1 Samuel 16, God told Samuel that he had chosen another person to be King of Israel and that he could be found living in the household of his father, Jesse, in Bethlehem, a city about four miles southwest of Jerusalem. While Samuel was unaware of this fact, Jesse had a formidable family—he had eight sons. Like a smart father, Jesse introduced Samuel first to his oldest son, Eliab, a big strapping young man whom Samuel thought would make a great king. But, Eliab was not God's choice. Neither were sons two and three, Abinadab and Shammah. In fact, Samuel met the first seven of Jesse's sons, none of whom were found to be God's chosen. O.K., so had Samuel heard God correctly? Where was the man who was supposed to be anointed as king? In one last-ditch effort, Samuel asked Jesse if he had any more sons lying around anywhere.

"Well," Jesse said, "I have one more son, my youngest, who is out tending the sheep." Obviously, this youngest son was not at the top of Jesse's list as king material—he wasn't even invited to the party to meet Samuel. Yet, when young David entered the house, the Lord said to Samuel, "This is the one…rise and anoint him." So Samuel took his container of oil, dumped it over David's head in the presence of his family, and anointed him the new King of Israel. While the oil of anointing was the visible sign that David was God's choice, we are told that, "From that day on the Spirit of the Lord came upon David in power" (1 Samuel 16:13).

What a dream! Two seconds before, David was just a shepherd boy. Now, his dream was to become a king.

David was now indisputably God's choice to be the next King of Israel. Of course this was an uneasy choice in the present king's view; as everyone knew the normal ascender to the throne should have been King Saul's son, Jonathan. But because the prophet of the Lord, Samuel, had made such a big deal of anointing David as the inheritor of the throne, and David responded to the calling of God by killing Israel's archenemy, Goliath, King Saul was hard-pressed to do anything other than acknowledge David as the heir apparent.

Almost more amazing than King Saul's recognition of David as the next king, was Jonathan's response. From the very first day the two men met, "Jonathan became one in spirit with David, and he loved him as himself...Jonathan took off the robe he was wearing and gave it to David, along with his tunic, and even his sword, his bow and his belt." All of these actions taken together indicated that Jonathan was, in effect, transferring his own status as heir to the throne to David. This was obviously not grudgingly done, but rather motivated by both love and respect from one man to another.

From that day forward, David was welcomed into the king's household, living under the tutelage of King Saul himself. What a great way for the future king to learn the ropes! Not only did David receive first-hand knowledge and experience in how to rule, but quite a relationship must have developed between these two men, their burgeoning closeness indicated by the fact that many times in scripture, David referred to King Saul as "Father." David's dream was actually going to be fulfilled!

David seemed to flourish in his new environment. Whatever King Saul asked David to do was accomplished with great success, even to the degree that King Saul gave David a high rank in the army, a move that "pleased all the people, and Saul's officers as well" (1 Samuel 18:5).

However, this idyllic relationship between King Saul and David lasted only as long as the battle against the Philistines and the march back to Jerusalem. The people living in that great city had evidently heard about David's success on the battlefield. Coming out to meet the returning troops, the people began to dance and sing in celebration of Israel's great victory: "Saul has slain his thousands, and David his tens of thousands" (1 Samuel 18:7). Uh oh. It's not a good thing for the young buck to look greater than the king. Sure enough, scripture says, "From that time on, Saul kept a jealous eye on David" (1 Samuel 18:9).

The very next day, David was in the palace playing his harp for the King, when Saul suddenly picked up a spear and hurled it at David, trying to pin him to the wall. When David eluded the spear the first time, Saul threw it once more, but again David dodged the spear. Thinking that God was somehow protecting David from him, Saul decided that the best thing to do was to send David away from his household and let others do the dirty deed. So, he gave David a thousand men, and basically told him to go out fight against Israel's enemies, hoping that David would die in the process.

So, how did David do? Not only didn't he die, but scripture says that, "in everything David did he had great success, because the Lord was with him" (1 Samuel 18:14).

King Saul just couldn't seem to get David dead! He couldn't kill David himself, and now even Israel's enemies couldn't kill him. But King Saul had another plan up his sleeve. His daughter, Michal, evidently was in love with David. Knowing that David was so poor that he couldn't possibly afford a dowry for Michal, Saul told David that he could have Michal for his wife if only he would kill one hundred Philistines in a battle. The Philistines were really big people—you remember the Philistine, Goliath? He was over nine feet tall! King Saul must have been thinking that if anyone could kill David, the Philistines could. So how did David do? He killed two hundred Philistines.

So now, King Saul had to give his daughter to David in marriage. This must have been incredibly galling to Saul; even though he had tried to kill him four separate times, not only was David still alive, his marriage to Michal gave him an even stronger tie to the throne! Not only was David's dream of becoming King of Israel still alive, he was even closer to the possibility with Michal at his side.

Increasingly more enraged at David's success, King Saul sent men to David's house to watch and wait for David to leave for the palace the next morning. Their orders were to kill David on sight. Somehow Michal heard about her father's plan and warned David that if he didn't run for his life that very night, Saul's men were going to kill him. So, Michal let David down to the ground through a window, and David escaped.

It was years before David was able to return home, his dream of becoming King of Israel all but dead.

David wrote Psalm 59 at this exact time in his life:

Deliver me from my enemies, O God; protect me from those who rise up against me. Deliver me from evildoers and save me from bloodthirsty men.

See how they lie in wait for me! Fierce men conspire against me for no offense or sin of mine, O LORD.
I have done no wrong, yet they are ready to attack me.
Arise to help me; look on my plight!
O my Strength, I watch for you; you, O God, are my fortress, my loving God.

They return at evening, snarling like dogs, and prowl about the city.

They wander about for food and howl if not satisfied.
But I will sing of your strength, in the morning I will sing of your love; for you are my fortress, my refuge in times of trouble.

O my Strength, I sing praise to you; you, O God, are my fortress, my loving God.

Notice that David referred to God as his "strength" three times, and his "fortress/refuge" four times in this Psalm. Understanding these two things about God was huge for David! With his escape from the "snarling dogs" under the cover of darkness, David was all by himself with no place to call "home." Take a closer look at how David views God as his strength and fortress:

The word "strength" is the Hebrew word *cōz*. This word is used primarily to describe God's strength, particularly in the Psalms. But not only is this strength a quality given by God, **He Himself** is that strength. David used this word throughout the Psalms to describe the security enjoyed by God's people. For example, "The Lord is a strong tower against the enemy" (Psalm 61:3) and "a mighty rock" (Psalm 62:7). The impartation of God's strength made David "secure as a strong mountain" (Psalm 30:7).

The word used in Psalm 59 for "fortress" is the word *miśgāb*. This word is derived from the root, *śagab* "to be high," and is found 15 times in the Old Testament, 11 of these found in the Psalms. *Miśgāb* speaks of God acting as a person's high tower (2 Samuel 22:3), or his refuge (Psalm 46:7, 11 [8, 12]), or defense (Isaiah 33:16). The allusion of "God-as-fortress" relates to the fact that in the ancient world, safety for the one fleeing from an enemy was synonymous with remaining upon some fortified height which would be inaccessible to beast and enemy alike. That is, being in a fortress meant one was safe. Another great thing about God-as-fortress, is that the word "fortress" is used in the emphatic sense in Psalm 59 and could therefore be translated, "The Lord is my fortress, **indeed!**"

When you add these two attributes of God together, "strength" and "fortress," we discover that David viewed God as this impregnable fortress set up on a high mountain where no one could get to him. This sounds like a pretty secure place to me, especially when you know an army is coming after you.

But, how did David deal with the death of his dream of becoming King? Let me just say that David's response to this disappointment was extraordinary. David said, not once in the Psalm, but twice, "I will sing praise." Are you kidding me? What about all of this could possibly evoke a song of praise?

Here's a story that will help give us some understanding of how we can actually praise God when a dream has died:

Very late one evening, I flipped on the television just in time to hear Oprah say, "So let's look back at Faith Hill." I **love** Faith Hill. She's beautiful and sings like nobody's business. Because it was 3:00 a.m., I thought Faith might be able to sing me into unconscious bliss so I could get a few hours of sleep before I had to face the day. But as the tape began to play of an earlier time in the history of the Oprah Winfrey show, I became quickly riveted to the TV set.

Oprah said to Faith, "Faith, I'd like to ask you to sing something you're probably not prepared to sing. You were singing something at the end of your rehearsal, and I'd like you to sing that song." Faith kind of blinked in astonishment. "You see," Oprah continued, "it's my favorite song. The name of the song is 'I Surrender All.'"

OK, now I'm really glued to the tube. Out of all of the songs on the planet, Oprah Winfrey's favorite is an old hymn?

"Now let me tell you why this is my favorite song," Oprah said. And, she began to tell the story.

When Oprah found out that Steven Spielberg was going to make a film from the book *The Color Purple*, the desire to be in that movie evidently overwhelmed her. In her own words, she had never wanted anything quite so badly in her whole life. So, she called everyone she knew who had any clout in Hollywood. She had never acted in a film before, but come on, she's Oprah Winfrey! Well, she finally got her foot in the door, but the powers that be actually required her to do a screen test. So, a screen test she did.

Well, a week went by, two weeks went by, and still she heard nothing. Into the third week, still not hearing a word, she took the matter into her own hands and called Spielberg's people. When she was finally connected with the right person, she was told quite tersely that she wouldn't be hired for the film because, "they have hired **real** actors to do the film."

Ouch! Not only did Oprah watch a dream die, she was devastated in the process.

Oprah said the only thing she could think to do was to just get away and try to deal with the hurt and disappointment. So, she got into her car and checked herself into a health spa (a.k.a., a "fat farm," she said). When she got there, she checked into her room, changed into her sweats, ran out to the track, and began to pray as her feet pounded on the packed dirt.

"God," she began, "This is just too heavy, too much for me to bear. I can't live with this disappointment. I wanted this so badly. Please, Lord, do something to lift this desire from my heart." So, Oprah ran and cried and prayed, and ran and cried and prayed. Suddenly, a song came to mind, so she began to sing and run and cry. The song?

All to Jesus, I surrender,
All to Him I freely give.
I will ever love and trust Him,
In His presence daily live.

I surrender all,
I surrender all.
All to thee my blessed Savior,
I surrender all.

With this song of praise to the God who is worthy of love and trust, Oprah let her dream die.

But something amazing happened in her heart while she was singing. "In a moment of time," Oprah said, "The Lord came down and just lifted the heaviness, and suddenly I was free; I was transformed." In a moment, God transformed the devastation of a dying dream into a supernatural peace.

About that time, the spa's receptionist ran out onto the track to tell Oprah that she had a phone call waiting for her. She was really irritated at the interruption and asked, "Do I really have to take this call?"

"Well, I don't know, Ms. Winfrey, but it's Steven Spielberg on the phone."

Running for all she was worth, she got to the phone to hear the voice at the other end of the line, "Oprah, if you still want that part it's yours. Oh, and by the way, are you at a fat farm? Don't lose one more ounce; this part calls for a stout woman."

Oprah said she hung up the phone, threw her stuff in the car, and after stopping at a Tastee Freez headed for home.

With that, Oprah stepped down from the stage, and Faith Hill began to sing *a capella*, "All to Jesus, I surrender…" The musicians joined in with her for the second verse, "All to Jesus, I surrender, humbly at His feet I bow. Worldly pleasures all forsaken, take me Jesus, take me now…"

As the third verse began, the back-up singers joined Faith, and the cameras began to pan the audience. "All to Jesus, I surrender, Lord, I give myself to Thee. Fill me with Thy love and power, let Thy blessing fall on me…"

A close-up of Oprah revealed tears running down her face, her hands lifted toward heaven; she was mouthing the words along with many in the audience who were now familiar with the song, "I surrender all, I surrender all. All to Jesus, blessed Savior, I surrender all."

It's a wonderful story, isn't it? Oprah no sooner let her dream die, than it was handed right back to her. As for David? It took about 22 years from the time he was anointed to be King of Israel to the time he actually became King, but become King he did.

And, oh, by the way…I ended up getting my Ph.D. from the University of Southern California and returning to my beloved alma mater as a real teacher, enabling me to give back to that wonderful community so much of what it had given me.

Letting your dream die may be excruciating now, but trust me—in the end God will take you way beyond your own dream into the dream He has for you.

WHEN I'M REALLY AFRAID

1 Samuel 21 & Psalm 34

The morning after my four-year-old nephew, Anthony, had a rather bad dream, I was deep into an explanation about how much more powerful God was than the boogie-man.

"You remember the stories about Jesus you've heard in Sunday School, don't you?" I asked. "Jesus has the power to heal people with leprosy. He has the power to walk on water," I said. "He even calmed a storm so big that it could have drowned all of his friends in the boat. Jesus is stronger than any bad dream! So," I said, "just tell the bad dream to go away in Jesus' name, and it will!" I could see by his eyes that I was making an impression. So I asked, "Do you understand?"

He looked at me for just a second then said, "I think so—Jesus is more powerful than all the Power Rangers put together!"

Well, so much for biblical exegesis to make my point. But the four-year-old did get it—Jesus really is greater than all of our fears. Yet, putting this knowledge into practice is not all that easy when we are facing one kind of terror or another.

Interestingly, the feeling of fear is a built-in part of human existence that is a positive experience. There is actually a part of our brain called the amygdala that secretes hormones that control fear and aggression. When we have a sense of fear, the amygdala releases hormones that put the human body into an "alert" state so that we are ready to move, run, fight, etc. This defensive "alert" state and our physical response to it is generally referred to in psychology as the "fight-or-flight" response. So, feeling fear is actually a good thing in many cases.

The polar side of healthy fear, however, is when the experience turns into what is known as a phobia. The word, "phobia" comes from the Greek word, *phobos*. This kind of fear is an irrational, intense, persistent fear of certain situations, activities, things, or people that results in an unreasonable desire to avoid that which is feared. When the fear is beyond one's control, or if the fear is interfering with daily life, then the phobia becomes an anxiety disorder. An American study by the National Institute of Mental Health (NIMH) found that between 8.7% and 18.1% of Americans suffer from phobias.

And, people can be afraid of some of the most amazing things. A few of the most unusual phobias include phalacrophobia—a fear of bald people; bibliophobia—a fear of books; sitophobia—a fear of eating; dikephobia—a fear of justice; and one of my personal favorites, pentheraphobia—a fear of mothers-in-law. While some of these fears can seem quite amusing, many people live their lives out in such fear that every decision they make and every relationship they have is directed by that fear.

While we can certainly understand the ongoing and extreme anxiety disorders that phobias bring, what most of us have to deal with, sometimes throughout our lives, is that kind of "middle ground" type of fear. You know—the fear we have of someone finding out who we really are, or the fear that we're not good enough. Once in a while, though, because of things like an illness or a tragic accident, we experience a moment in time when fear almost overwhelms us – these are the times when we face such fear that all we want to do is run from the situation that's causing the fear.

How in the world do we deal with this kind of fear? Take a look at David during a moment in his life when he faced absolute terror.

Spending all your time running for your life is not really any kind of life at all. Yet, this is exactly what King-in-waiting David was relegated to. In fact, chapter 19 of 1 Samuel records the final break in the relationship between King Saul and David. Look at the vocabulary found in that chapter: "go into hiding," "eluded," "made good his escape," "run for your life," "fled and escaped," "escaped," "get away," "fled and made his escape."

When the King wants to kill you and has access to an entire army, there really are not many places to hide. David was smart, though. If there was a place of safety at all, David reasoned, it would have to be with the man of God who anointed him King—even King Saul was afraid of Samuel.

So, David ran to Ramah where Samuel lived. When David told Samuel that King Saul wanted to kill him, he and Samuel went to Naioth where a group of prophets lived and stayed with them for a time. But it wasn't long before Saul found out where David was hiding and sent men after him. In fact, Saul dispatched three contingents of soldiers to kill him. When the first group of Saul's soldiers arrived, they saw the assembly of prophets "prophesying," or delivering prophetic oracles, and the "spirit of God came upon Saul's men." Instead of killing David, they too prophesied. When he heard of this, Saul sent a second delegation, which broke out into prophesy just like the first group. A third group experienced the same thing.

At this point, King Saul, himself, went to Naioth. "But the Spirit of God came even upon him, and he walked along prophesying" (1 Samuel 19:23), also failing to kill David. Having miraculously escaped with his life, David then fled from Samuel the prophet in Naioth, and ran to Ahimelech, the priest living in Nob.

When David arrived in Nob, the first thing he asked Ahimelech for was not sanctuary, but rather, bread; hunger, in this case, actually outweighed safety! So, Ahimelech gave David the bread that had been removed from the altar of the Lord the day before. His first request met, David did an unusual thing: he asked Ahimelech for a weapon. I'm not sure that the local synagogue is actually the place one would go to find a weapon, but miraculously, Ahimelech did indeed have a weapon. And, what a weapon it was! It happened to be the sword of Goliath. How this sword ended up in Nob is anyone's guess. The last reference to it, after David had used it to cut off the Philistine's head (1 Samuel 17:51), was the notice that David had put the giant's armor in his own tent. Yet, here the famous sword was, just when David really needed it.

So, with his stomach full and Goliath's sword at his side, David fled to Achish the King of Gath. Gath, ironically, was a Philistine city and was Goliath's hometown. Why, exactly, David went to this particular city is not really known, but it could have been that he was hoping to become anonymous in this very large city, looking to be hired on as an ordinary mercenary soldier. For whatever reason, David found himself at the gate of the Philistine's capital city. If David wanted to arrive incognito and blend in with the other guys who also were armored up and ready to go, his plan really went south; he was immediately recognized by some of Achish's soldiers. In fact, several soldiers went so far as to begin to mock David. "Isn't this David, the 'King' of the land?" they laughed. "Isn't this the guy they sing about, 'Saul has slain his thousands, and David his tens of thousands? (1 Samuel 29:5).'"

How did David respond to being recognized and mocked by these soldiers? By being absolutely scared to death! David had to be thinking about how in the world he was going to be able to get himself out of this situation without getting killed. It seems to me that David could have talked himself out of the situation by simply playing "the enemy of my enemy is my friend" game with Achish. Achish surely would have realized the powerful ally he would have found in David had they joined together, even if only for a while. But, no. Instead, David was totally terrified.

Now, think about this… David, anointed King of Israel, standing at the gate of the Philistine capitol city **with Goliath's sword in his hand**. Come on! You'd think that David would merely look at the sword and remember how he had gotten that sword in the first place and in doing so, regain all the courage he needed. You remember the story, don't you? It is recorded in 1 Samuel 17.

The first time young David saw Goliath, the giant stood nearly ten feet tall, his armor alone weighed 126 pounds; he wore a bronze helmet on his beach ball-sized head and bronze shin guards on his muscular legs. In addition to a bronze sword strapped to his side, Goliath carried a spear that was as big as a fence rail with the tip that weighed more than 15 pounds.

And on the other side was Israel's army, all arrayed against Goliath and the Philistine army: the Israelites on one hill, the Philistines on the opposing hill, with only a valley between the two armies.

Every day for forty days, Goliath would walk down his hill, into the valley and stand before the entire Israelite army. "Pick your best soldier and pit him against me," he'd bellow. "If he gets the upper hand and kills me, the Philistines will all become your slaves. But if I get the upper hand and kill him, you'll all become our slaves and serve us. I challenge the troops of Israel this day," he would roar. "Give me a man. Let us fight it out together!"

For forty days! For nearly a month and a half Israel's army stood there and listened to this Arnold Schwarzenegger-on-steroids taunt them. And how did Israel respond? Scripture says, "They were terrified and lost all hope" (1 Samuel 17:4).

On the fortieth day, Jesse told his teen-aged son, David, to run and take food to his brothers who were serving in Israel's army. Evidently, David stayed around the camp that day long enough to hear Goliath's challenge. David asked, "What's in it for the man who kills that Philistine and gets rid of this ugly blot on Israel's honor? Who does he think he is anyway, this ungodly Philistine, taunting the armies of God?"

No sooner had he gotten the question out of his mouth than David's oldest brother, Eliab flew at him. "What are you doing here!" he yelled. "Why aren't you minding your own business, tending that scrawny flock of sheep?"

But one of the other soldiers answered David's question. "The man who kills the giant will have it made! The King will give him a huge reward," he said, "offer his daughter as a bride and take care of his entire family for life!"

Well, King Saul soon heard what this young man was saying about Goliath and sent for David. "Master," David said, "don't give up hope. I'm ready to go and fight the Philistine."

"Oh, man," King Saul sniggered. "You can't go and fight this Philistine. You're too young and inexperienced. This guy's been fighting since before you were born."

David boldly replied, "Listen. I've been a shepherd tending sheep for my father. Whenever a lion or bear came and took a lamb from the flock, I'd go after it, knock it down, and rescue the lamb. If it turned on me, I'd grab it by the throat, wring its neck, and kill it. Lion or bear," David declared, "it made no difference—I just killed it. And I'll do the same to the Philistine pig who is taunting God's army. God, who delivered me from the teeth of the lion and the claws of the bear, will deliver me from the Philistine."

"OK," Saul said. "Go, and God help you!" Hoping to give him every advantage, Saul outfitted David with his own armor. But when David tried to walk, the armor was so heavy, that he said, "I can't even move in this stuff." So, off came the armor. He then picked out five smooth stones from the bank of the nearby brook, grabbed his sling and his shepherd's staff, and off he went to face Goliath.

Goliath had been pacing back and forth, waiting to see if anyone from Israel's army would take him up on the challenge. About this time, the giant looked down and saw peach-fuzz-faced David standing there with his shepherd's staff in hand. "Am I a dog that you come after me with a stick?" Goliath sneered. "Come on," he taunted, "I'll make road kill of you for the buzzards. I'll turn you into a tasty morsel for the field mice!"

"Hah!" David said. "You come at me with sword and spear. I come at you in the name of God, the God of Israel's army, whom you curse and mock. This very day God is handing you over to me. I'm about to kill you and cut off your head and serve your body and the bodies of your Philistine buddies to the crows. The whole earth will know that there's an amazing God in Israel…The battle belongs to God and he's handing you to us on a platter!"

With that, Goliath started toward David, and David took off running toward Goliath. The boy grabbed a stone from his pocket, slung it, and hit Goliath so hard, that it embedded itself in Goliath's forehead. Down the Philistine crashed, face first, into the dirt. David finished the job by pulling Goliath's sword out of its sheath and using it to cut off Goliath's head.

David's victory over Goliath was not merely a story of the underdog winning a surprising conquest, but was also the initial confirmation of David's anointing as King. This victory was supposed to be the foundation of David's reign: the reminder that no matter what enemy David faced, for the rest of his life, God's miraculous power would deliver him. How could David not have remembered all of this?

Yet there he was, standing at the Philistine city's gate with Goliath's sword in hand—the great reminder of what he had accomplished in God's name just a few years earlier. Did David challenge the Philistine guard in God's name? Did he even pull out a sling and a smooth stone? Nope. When David, God's great warrior—the killer of lions, bears and giants—realized that he had been recognized, he was so afraid for his life that he chose to begin staggering around, shrieking and clawing at the gate with his fingernails! He babbled and let saliva run down his beard; acting the part of a man gone totally insane (1 Samuel 21:13).

In just one moment of time, David the Feared became David the Fearful.

When Achish saw this, he exclaimed to his servants, "Don't I have enough madmen in my own household as it is without wanting to bring this guy here as well?" And with that declaration, David was booted out of Gath. David ran for about ten miles that day, finding a cave in the foothills of Judah in which to hide.

Utterly exhausted, scared out of his wits and humiliated down to the core of his being, David hunkered down in the cave of Adullum and wrote Psalm 34. David wrote:

> *I will extol the LORD at all times; his praise will always be on my lips.*
> *My soul will boast in the LORD; let the afflicted hear and rejoice.*
> *Glorify the LORD with me; let us exalt his name together.*
> *I sought the LORD, and he answered me; he delivered me from all my fears.*
> *Those who look to him are radiant; their faces are never covered with shame.*
> *This poor man called, and the LORD heard him; he saved him out of all his troubles.*
> *The angel of the LORD encamps around those who fear him, and he delivers them.*
> *Taste and see that the LORD is good; blessed is the man who takes refuge in him.*
> *Fear the LORD, you his saints, for those who fear him lack nothing.*
> *The lions may grow weak and hungry, but those who seek the LORD lack no good thing.*
> *Come, my children, listen to me; I will teach you the fear of the LORD*
> *. . . The righteous cry out, and the LORD hears them; he delivers them from all their troubles.*

*The LORD is close to the brokenhearted and saves those who
are crushed in spirit.
A righteous man may have many troubles, but the LORD
delivers him from them all.
. . The LORD redeems his servants; no one will be condemned
who takes refuge in him.*

The first couple of lines in the Psalm may, at first glance, seem really incongruent with what David was actually feeling, especially because we have the idea that praising God like this is reserved for times when everything is going great. In truth, there is no greater praise for God than that which occurs when you have escaped a volatile situation with all of your limbs intact. This was a "Thank you, THANK YOU, God, for hearing my cry and getting me out of this mess" kind of praise that David was giving God. More interesting here is that David was not praising God for delivering him from death by the hand of King Achish, but rather for delivering him **from all of his fears**.

The word for "fear" here is the Hebrew word *meguwrah*. The root of this word means "to be intimidated before a stronger or superior being or thing." This is the kind of fear that leads to abject terror, and God's deliverance from this kind of fear was so complete for David that he says his face was no longer "covered with shame." I'm sure David was remembering the shame he felt as spittle ran over his face and he attempted to appear insane.

God's deliverance from fear not only removes the fear itself, but also removes the shame that fear generates. Think about how huge this kind of freedom from fear is! I have a sign on my desk that asks this question: "What would you attempt to do if you had no fear of failure?" This question leads to a major point.

God miraculously delivering us from the person or thing we fear is not simply the removal of all fear. As we discussed earlier, some fears are healthy: they keep us from making bad decisions; they keep us from hurting others or ourselves. Therefore, simply removing fear from our life experience would not be all that positive—in fact, it would put us in harm's way to a greater degree. God delivers us from fear by teaching us **who** to fear and **how** to fear. How does this work?

In this short Psalm, David used the phrase, "fear the Lord," and "fear Him" no less than four times! So, whom do we fear? God Himself. The word for "fear" David uses these four times is a different Hebrew word than he used earlier in the Psalm. The word here is *yare'* and it means to have a sense of "awe" or "reverence." When you revere someone, you respect and admire that person. Sometimes you may be amazed by this person, but you are never terrorized by them. This, obviously, is a different kind of fear altogether.

For David, this kind of fear, or better, reverence, of the Lord was the basis upon which all human wisdom was built. In another Psalm, David declared, "The fear of the Lord is the beginning of wisdom" (Psalm 111:10). This means that the respect and admiration, and even the total amazement, for God implied by the word "fear" will actually have the effect of creating within us the fertile ground in which all of our lives grow and are developed. To revere, admire and respect God means that our lives are singularly focused on our relationship with Him, the wisest way one can live life. This kind of fear of God will always lead to more trust and more faith in the one who is able to bring joy and fulfillment to our lives.

On the other hand, to live one's life in constant terror of an Achish can easily result in an attempt to cover up our fear by trying to become feared by others, like the big bully in the school yard. A second potential outcome of living in constant terror is becoming absolutely paralyzed by our fear, thereby allowing it to turn into a full-fledged phobia. Either of these responses to fear will allow fear to rule over us with every relationship, every decision, even every dream.

But look what David suggested we do: "Fear the Lord, you his saints, for those who fear him lack nothing. The lions may grow weak and hungry, but those who seek the Lord lack no good thing" (Psalm 34:9, 10). David first declared that those who fear or revere the Lord can depend on God for the provision of their basic needs—they will lack no good thing.

By way of contrast, David said that the "young lions" do lack and grow hungry. The lion metaphor is really powerful. Of all the animals, the proverbial "King of the Jungle" is viewed as the most powerful and least likely to lack prey and go hungry. At the core of its being, the lion is a predator and is feared over most every other animal. There comes a time, however, when even the lion will face times of hunger. What then? While those who fear the Lord can turn to God for help, to whom can a predator turn for help?

But wait—doesn't the reality of David's life actually contradict what he has been saying in the Psalm?

Remember where David was? He was totally by himself, hiding like an animal in a cave. In spite of his circumstance, read what David said about his plight! "Taste and see," he said, "that the Lord is good. Blessed is the man who takes refuge in Him." It may have been a physical cave in which David was hiding, but David understood that God Himself was his true place of safety. The fear of the Lord was indeed the foundation of life for David, and even the key to experiencing joy in life. But the fear of the Lord is not a guarantee that life will be always easy, devoid of the difficulties that bring so much pain. Look at how David ended Psalm 34:

> *The LORD is close to the brokenhearted and saves those who*
> *are crushed in spirit.*
> *A righteous man may have many troubles, but the LORD*
> *delivers him from them all*
> (vv 18-19).

The reality is that a good person (a righteous man) may have many troubles; David certainly did. But while the fear of the Lord will not always prevent the heart from being broken, it will work to mend the broken heart; we will not always avoid the forces that create devastation in our lives, but fearing the Lord will restore the spiritually crushed. God's presence is experienced *within* these crisis situations; David understood that there is no divine guarantee that the righteous will escape the crises and trials of our existence.

No one gets to avoid the difficulties of life altogether, yet the fear of the Lord does carry with it the promise of divine protection; God does watch over the physical welfare of His people and protect them. David was not naïve. Look what this man had been through up to that point! What

David was assured of, according to Psalm 34, is that though much of his life had been characterized by hardship and difficulty, the fear of the Lord always brought with it God's divine presence which made victory possible in the midst of trial.

A story is told of a man and his young son who were playing in a park when a bombardment of London began during World War II. With absolutely no shelter from the falling bombs, the father, in a flash of insight, decided that the possibility of two bombs falling in exactly the same place was astronomically high. So he grabbed his young son and ran to the lip of a bomb crater, set his son down on the ground, and leaped off the edge into the bottom of the newly formed crater. He scrambled up to his feet, and reaching as high as he could he yelled, "Hurry, son, jump! I'll catch you!" His son looked down into the hole and screamed, "But Dad, it's so deep and a bomb might fall on us. We need to run!"

"Don't be afraid! Trust me, son," the dad yelled back. "JUMP! NOW!" The little boy, trusting his dad with all of his heart, took a flying leap off the crater's edge, landing in his dad's arms. The dad covered his son with his own body, safely hidden until the bombs ceased to fall.

Notice what David declares near the end of his 34th Psalm: "A righteous man may have many troubles," David said, "but the LORD delivers him from them all. . .The LORD redeems his servants; no one will be condemned who takes refuge in him "(Psalm 34:19,22).

For some of us in the middle of some kind of spiritual or physical war, a bomb crater looks like the least safe place to be. But our awesome Heavenly Father has the ability and the desire to relieve us from fearing the Achishes in our lives by reminding us that He is the God who protects us and delivers us. How does God remind us of this amazing ability? Look at what's in your hand! It may not be Goliath's sword you see your hand grasping, but it will be something just like it. Remember the times that God has been faithful in your life and gave you the ability to defeat giants? When he provided for you in a miraculous way? When you received direction just when you needed it? Take your refuge in God; He will deliver you from all of your fears!

Chapter

WHEN LIFE ISN'T FAIR

Psalm 54/1 Samuel 23

A good friend of mine has rheumatoid arthritis. When she first told me she had RA, I honestly thought that the disease was just the regular old arthritis all of us will eventually suffer from when we get older, perhaps only worse somehow. But no—what I learned is that rheumatoid arthritis is actually a virus that affects a person's autoimmune system. When someone has RA, the body's tissues are mistakenly attacked by its own immune system. Patients with autoimmune diseases have antibodies in their blood that target their own body tissues, causing joint destruction and functional disability. The joint inflammation of rheumatoid arthritis causes swelling, pain, stiffness, and redness in the joints. The inflammation of rheumatoid disease can also occur in tissues around the joints, such as the tendons, ligaments, and muscles.

When my friend awakes in the morning, she gingerly gets out of bed, slowly rises to her feet, and painfully duck-walks into the restroom. This, she tells me, is because during the last few months the RA has created such swelling in her knees that she can't straighten her legs. Some days, she says, her hands and wrists are in so much pain that she has a hard time holding onto a toothbrush or a comb. It's like walking around with a 101° fever—every day.

There are several drugs people with RA can take in order to stem the disease's affects. All of them work to suppress the immune system. This means that the immune system will stop attacking good tissue; it also means that the RA patient is much more vulnerable to the other viruses lingering out there. And, while some drugs will help some RA patients, those same drugs will have no effect for others. This makes treating RA patients a kind of hit-and-miss procedure; you try one drug and wait six to eight weeks to see if it yields favorable results. If not, you move to a different drug. The obvious trouble with this method is that if the drug ends up not working, the RA patient has perhaps up to eight weeks of the disease running rampant in the body, allowing the full agony to make itself known. And while RA has its ebbs and flows, this is her life—agony of some sort. In spite of the constant pain, my friend is actually pretty up-beat about life. She's had to make many adjustments to her life, some big, some small, in order to accommodate her illness, but she still finds great joy in life. Yet, she told me one day, "It's not that I want to just die—ending my own life is NEVER an option. It's just that it takes so much energy to just keep living."

To clarify, I'm not talking about people who want to end their own lives. Rather, I'm talking about people who are in a constant day-to-day struggle because their circumstances make life hard to live. Overcoming drug addiction or alcoholism; the constant agony of a difficult marriage; the rub of children not living up to their potential; not having the money to make ends meet—I'm talking about the day, after day, after day strains of life that sometimes seem too hard to negotiate, and sometimes make one wonder if the effort is really worth the trouble...the days when life is just not fair.

While the issue with King-in-waiting David was not a physical one like my friend's RA, this young man also found himself in a constant, day-after-day struggle to live. To understand the incredible moment-by-moment stress that David experienced, imagine being relentlessly pursued by the CIA because the President has given the order to kill you on sight! This was David's everyday challenge – just staying ahead of the 'CIA'.

While trying to hide from King Saul's elite army, David gathered a following of men who believed that he really should be King of Israel. Of course, this didn't make things any easier for David. It wouldn't be too difficult for one person to find a hiding place and feed himself, but when you've got a couple hundred guys on the run with you, the logistic nightmare would multiply exponentially. I wonder if after a while David himself questioned whether becoming King of Israel was worth all the effort and stress. In fact, up until the point when David was anointed by God to be King of Israel, he had never had this much trouble in his life! He must have thought back with great fondness to his carefree days of tending sheep on the hillsides of Bethlehem, where there was always enough food to eat, and nothing but the occasional wild animal to fear.

So it was just after King Saul had destroyed the entire city of Nob including all of its inhabitants that David, who was hiding out in the vast desert near Nob, was told that the Philistines, Israel's old arch-enemy, were fighting against the people living in nearby Keilah—a Jewish city located in the western foothills of Judah. This meant that the armies of Israel were fighting on two fronts; King Saul had committed hundreds of his soldiers to take down Nob, so the people of Keilah knew King Saul was too far away to come to their rescue. Besides, if King Saul had just killed all of the inhabitants of one Jewish city, why would he come to the rescue of another? This was a dire time for the people of Keilah. With what few soldiers there were, along with the citizens of the city, they were on their own in attempting to rebuff the Philistine's attack.

As a result, the battle was not going well for the Keilahites. The Philistines were not only fighting them in hand-to-hand combat, but they were also "looting their threshing floors," (or in other words, stealing all of the grain the people had stored up for future use). You get the idea that if there was anyone left alive after the Philistines' siege of Keilah, the people remaining would surely have been left to die of hunger.

David must have felt compassion for the citizens of Keilah; he knew they really had no one to turn to for help. I think it was probably in David's heart to help them, but coming out of hiding in the desert would mean that he would have the Philistine army in front of him and King Saul's army behind him—not a very secure position by any means. Pinned between his two largest threats, he asked the Lord if he should take his crew of 400 men and wage war against the Philistine army. (There's something about divine guidance that gives one courage to face the difficult.) To his inquiry, the Lord answered, "Go and attack."

Great! David has the word of the Lord to attack, which was tantamount to God's promise of success in the endeavor. Going into battle would not be quite so difficult when you are more or less guaranteed success.

Unfortunately, David's men didn't take the news so well. When he told his small army what the Lord had commanded them to do, the men responded with total fear. "We're afraid enough as it is just trying to steer clear of Saul," they said. "We'd be absolutely terrified to go up against the Philistines."

So, David inquired of the Lord a second time, just to make sure he had heard correctly. This time the Lord commanded David, "Go down to Keilah, for I am going to give the Philistines into your hand." In other words, God was clearly saying, "Read my lips, David. I will give you victory over the Philistines." Sure enough, when David and his army of 400 attacked the Philistines, there were heavy losses in the enemy's ranks. The Philistines were so utterly defeated that David's army was even able to carry off all of their food supply.

The trouble with winning a battle against the Philistines, however, is that you tend to get a lot of press out of it. That being said, it wasn't long before King Saul heard that David and his rag-tag army had settled in Keilah. And of course, the king could not have been more ecstatic about this news! Keilah was surrounded by walls and had only two gates, with a bar to hold them in place, at the entrance of the city—one way in and one way out. "Ah ha!" King Saul must have thought, "David has imprisoned himself. Now I've got him without a doubt!" Saul began to move his 4,000 troops toward Keilah.

When David discovered that King Saul was rallying his army, David once again sought guidance from the Lord. This time, David was concerned about the loyalty of the citizens of Keilah. Were they loyal to King Saul, or were they loyal to David? Should he trust the Keilahites to provide a place of sanctuary for him, or would they surrender him to King Saul without a second thought? The Lord verified David's suspicions with the simple confirmation: "They will surrender you to Saul."

So then, David took his men and "kept moving from place to place." In fact, when David left Keilah, he fled to the Desert of Ziph, then to the Desert of Maon, and finally ended up in the strongholds of En Gedi.

OK, this was definitely not fair! A quick recap: David had just saved an entire city from the Philistines, and what did the people do? Give him a feast; honor him with awards; offer him a haven of safety where he could rest from battle? No. God warned David that the citizens of Keilah would certainly betray him, so off David and his army went, without even a pat on the back or a word of thanks.

To make things even worse, it didn't take long for King Saul to intensify the search for David and his men. In fact, while David was in the

Desert of Ziph, scripture says that, "Day after day Saul searched for him," with Saul vowing that, "if he is in the area, I will track him down" (1 Samuel 23:14, 23). In addition to the pressure of hiding from Saul, when the Ziphites discovered that David and his men were hiding in their land, they went directly to Saul saying, "Is not David hiding among us?" and offered to hand David over to him (1 Samuel 23:19-20). Saul thought this was just a wonderful idea, and asked the Ziphites to find out exactly where David was hiding. So, now you've got Saul's army and the Ziphites tracking down David and his men.

Feeling the pressure from these two sides, David and his army ran to the Desert of Maon. David was only a step ahead of Saul, however. Scripture says that, "Saul was going along one side of the mountain, and David and his men were on the other side, hurrying to get away from Saul" (1 Samuel 23:26). Whew! This really was too close for comfort! But, just as Saul and his forces were closing in on David and his men to capture them, a messenger came to Saul, saying, "Come quickly! The Philistines are raiding the land." So, Saul broke off his pursuit of David and went to meet the Philistines.

While it may seem as if David and his men got a reprieve, there are a few things to take into consideration. David, King-in-waiting, **was still** running for his life—-and for the lives of the 600 men who had joined with him by this time. They had just fought a battle, and there were still many critically wounded soldiers in need of care. Of course, there was also the arduous task of feeding and finding water for this 600—while in the desert, no less! So, not only was David wondering what was going on in his own life, he also had the responsibility of herding and hiding faithful followers.

Talk about life becoming too much! Constant stress, constant pressure, not knowing what the next day would bring – or even if there would be a next day. This was, in no way, what David thought his life would be when he was anointed King. Where was the glory? The wealth? The prestige? And living the life of an outlaw in the desert, tired, dirty, and hungry? It was just not fair!

Yet it was during this time that David wrote Psalm 54. It's a rather short Psalm, only seven verses long, probably because David wrote it while on the run:

> *Save me, O God, by your name; vindicate me by your might.*
> *Hear my prayer, O God; listen to the words of my mouth.*
> *Strangers are attacking me; ruthless men seek my life—men*
> *without regard for God. Selah*
> *Surely God is my help; the Lord is the one who sustains me.*
> *Let evil recoil on those who slander me; in your faithfulness*
> *destroy them.*
> *I will sacrifice a freewill offering to you; I will praise your*
> *name, O LORD, for it is good.*
> *For he has delivered me from all my troubles, and my eyes*
> *have looked in triumph on my foes.*

Look at David's language: 'Save me!' 'Vindicate me!' 'Hear me!' These sound like the words of a truly desperate man, a man at the end of his rope.

In the midst of all of his angst, David declared that God was his "help." The word for "help" that David used here is the Hebrew word, *'azar* and it literally means, "to rescue" and "to save." Interestingly, this word was used only 80 times in the entire Old Testament and almost exclusively described military assistance. During this time of multiple attempts on David's life, there was one thing that he definitely learned: God always has the ability to rescue him and save him.

David also understood that the Lord is the one who "sustains" him. This was the Hebrew word, *sānak*. The primary meaning of this word is "to lean upon," or "to rest one's self upon."

It is vital to understand here that it is impossible to "rest one's self upon" the Lord unless you first discover that God will "rescue and save." The ability to rest on the Lord is totally reliant on the fact that you truly believe God will rescue you, especially when life isn't fair.

How did David experience God's rest and rescue? God sent David some help from a very unlikely source—Jonathan, the son of the man who was trying to kill him. 1 Samuel 23:16-18 says:

> *And Saul's son Jonathan went to David at Horesh and helped him find strength in God. "Don't be afraid," he said. "My father Saul will not lay a hand on you. You will be king over Israel, and I will be second to you. Even my father Saul knows this." The two of them made a covenant before the LORD.*

Just when David is about to lose it, here came his old friend, Jonathan, to encourage him. I really don't know how Jonathan found David when his father, King Saul, was unable to. Nor do I know how Jonathan even made it through the sentries guarding David. But made it he did—just in the nick of time.

Scripture says that Jonathan encouraged David "in God." When writers of scripture use the prepositional phrase "in God" or "in Christ" the word "in" always refers to a place, a sphere of existence. Jonathan didn't simply fill David's ear with platitudes; nor did he merely pat him on the back and tell him that everything would be OK. Instead, he reminded David that while he was physically running for his life in the desert, totally worn out and wondering what in the world was going on, David's true existence was found **in** God! Even though he might not have been aware of it, God's presence was surrounding David all the while, and that presence worked to assure David that God's will would be accomplished. That's why Jonathan was able to say, "Don't be afraid...You **will** be King."

One incredibly wonderful thing to know about God is that He doesn't just sit on His throne in heaven, making amazing (and somewhat impossible) declarations about our futures, then joke to Himself, "I'll just wait to see if these poor humans can really make any of this happen." While your situation may be so difficult that you can't seem to feel His presence, God **is** with you and **is** totally involved in your circumstance, empowering you and strengthening you moment by moment. You can always trust God to bring you through your circumstance, and **especially** during those times when life isn't fair.

I love to watch the Olympic Games. Every few years the greatest athletes from around the globe meet together to compete in some of the most physically demanding sports of our time. Of course "winning the gold" has to be the most amazing personal experience any athlete can imagine, but they don't seem to do what they do solely for personal glory. This competition is about performing as a representative of one's country, and this, I think, is what accounts for the tears on the winners' faces. As they stand before the world with their gold medals around their necks and their national anthem playing, their country's flag is raised to the top of the very highest pole.

While every Olympic sport is intriguing, I love to watch the runners. Every movement they make is compact and purposeful in their drive to the finish line. It really is poetry in motion.

In 1992, the Olympians met in Barcelona, Spain. Glued to my television set, I watched every race, thinking each one better than the last. The hours I spent there seemed to quietly melt away.

It was a race in the late afternoon: eight runners lined up at the starting blocks preparing for the 400-meter semifinal race. Among those participating was a young Brit by the name of Derek Redmond.

The television commentators began to explain to the viewers why this particular person's appearance at the Olympics was quite miraculous. Evidently, he had undergone a total of eight surgeries between the 1988 Olympics and his appearance on that day. The last of these surgeries was the mending of a torn Achilles tendon, occurring less than four months before the Barcelona Games! In spite of the fact that everyone had told him there was absolutely no way he could possibly compete, Redmond continued his training as best he could—on one leg, believing all the while that he would be in shape in time for the Games.

As he headed into the Barcelona Olympics, Redmond seemed to be doing quite well physically. This was immediately apparent when he posted the fastest time of the first round of the competition and then went on to win his quarterfinal race. What a man! While Redman had entered the Olympics as a huge underdog, his performance in the first two heats of the 400-meter race quickly gave him the reputation of a superman.

Then, it was time for the semifinals. All of the racers toed their mark, the gun went off, and the eight ran for all they were worth. Everything looked great for Derek Redmond. He virtually leapt from the starting block, and quickly found himself leading the pack. But about half way around the course, Redmond pulled up—stopping suddenly. He hopped on one leg and then dropped to the ground. Along with millions of other viewers, my heart sank as I thought, "Oh, no! His Achilles tendon!" (As it turned out, it wasn't his Achilles tendon, but a different injury altogether—a torn hamstring, an excruciating injury.)

The television cameras panned around to Redmond, focusing in slowly. The look of anguish on the man's face was heart-rending. You could see the agony of the injury, and you could feel the disappointment. He had now lost his final chance at an Olympic medal. Tears mingled with sweat and dripped off his cheeks as he pulled himself to his feet and took a hop forward. Then, another hop forward. Stretcher-bearers rushed toward him, but he waved them off, taking yet another hop. It finally dawned on us that Redmond was determined to finish the race. Another hop! By this time, I'm sure I wasn't the only one yelling at the television set, "Come on, Derek! You can do it!"

Suddenly, a man came running from the stands, making a beeline toward Redmond on the track. There were a couple of 300-pound security guards trying to catch him, but just as the mysterious fellow reached

Redmond, one of the TV commentators took notice, yelling, "Oh my goodness! It looks like Jim Redmond, Derek's father, has run out onto the field!"

The TV camera, now zoomed in on Redmond and his dad, allowed the audience to barely lip-read the words he spoke to his son: "Derek, it's your Dad."

Derek turned to his father and said, "Dad, I've got to finish this race."

"Then son," his father replied, "we'll do it together."

Jim Redmond reached around his son's waist, half-carrying Derek toward the finish line, urging his son on all the while. "Come on son, we can do this," he encouraged. "You're not by yourself, Derek. We'll do this together. Come on son. Just a few more yards. Lean on me, Derek; we'll make it together."

Isn't it amazing that in the midst of great stress, wading waist-deep in trouble and sorrow, thinking we can't go on one more day, here comes Father God into the arena of our lives, putting his arm around us and saying, "Come on, child. We can do this; you're not by yourself; we'll make it together." You get it, don't you? Rest and rescue is possible in the midst of unfair circumstances simply because God is in the situation with us.

In honesty, the demanding circumstances of David's life didn't change after his meeting with Jonathan—he was forced to continue running from his enemy. He did so, however, with the great confidence that his enemy would never gain the upper hand. David knew that one day he would be King.

As for Derek Redmond, he did finish the race! 65,000 people stood on their feet for a whole ten minutes cheering him—the longest standing ovation in Olympic history. Hardly anyone remembers who actually won the gold medal, but everyone remembers the young man who leaned on his father and crossed the finish line… in spite of life not being fair.

WHEN I WANT REVENGE

1 Samuel 24 – Psalm 142

Y ou may have a tough time believing this, but there are several websites that actually give instructions for how to best get revenge on someone. Several of these sites have a section that allows people to share their revenge stories. Let's just say unless you want a vengeful mom wreaking havoc on your life, don't mess with her kids. If you're really serious about revenge, then there's even a site where you can buy voodoo dolls, and for a few extra dollars they will teach you some retribution spells and curses to use against your enemies.

One of the websites has a list of creative ideas for revenge-getting. Here are a few, in the avenger's own words and punctuation:

1. During the winter, plow snow in front of your enemy's garage. It's kind of funny when they can't get their car out.

2. Go to your local pet shop and buy some pests or get a hold of some somehow. Roaches are the most fun since they scatter in light. Flies are cool too since they would lay eggs... Send them a package with some sort of food (fruitcake works well) and add your pests.

3. Make a bumper sticker that says something to the nature of "white power, Jesus is dead, anything about weed smoking for the cops, KKK rules...etc" and put it on your enemy's bumper. I wonder how long they would drive around before they figure out it is there????? HAHA!

Then there's the story of the guy who wanted to get back at his girlfriend; he said, "I bought four BIG cans of tuna fish in OIL (Important). Took them home, and drained them into a jar. Took the jar to my ex-girlfriend's work and slowly and carefully poured the fishy smelling oil down the passenger side air intake of her new car (between the windshield and hood). This is the side that the heater core is on all cars. Once this smelly oil gets into the core, for the rest of the life of the car, the smell of rotten fish will never go away. And it gets worse with time."

While these illustrations may be humorous in a warped kind of way, they are still destructive. And, all too often, the desire for revenge can lead to a violent conclusion. The murder of an ex-spouse over a new boyfriend, gang shootings, bride burnings in India, throwing acid on a disobedient wife's face in Africa are all indicators of a world-wide epidemic of violence caused by the desire for revenge. These kinds of actions, at the very least, fly in the face of what it means to love an enemy, and in the final conclusion can make the avenger more legally culpable than the enemy.

What is it that makes revenge so appealing to us? Leland R. Beaumont suggests that the desire for revenge originates from the primal need for self-defense; a kind of cave man you-hurt-me, I'll-hurt-you-back law (Beaumont, 2005-2009). In today's world, however, where we actually have strong civil laws in place, the desire for revenge seems to occur when we feel as if we have been attacked and have, as a result, suffered some unjust loss or injury. We seek revenge when any of the following occur:

- We feel the need to act on feelings of anger, hate, jealousy or envy;
- We feel a real sense of humiliation, especially if someone has made us feel, foolish, ridiculous, stupid, or ashamed;
- We feel a need to "defend our honor" or the honor of our family, ancestors, or some other group with whom we identify.

No matter which of these reasons is the basis for an act of revenge, the goal is always to erase personal and and to restore one's sense of self-respect.

The real question is: Does revenge actually have the desired effect? Is the anticipated sense of satisfaction one may possibly get from the ultimate pay-back really worth hurting or humiliating the one who hurt you? Does revenge actually work to erase our humiliation and shame and restore our confidence?

Well, we're about to look at a circumstance in would-be-King David's life that is a great illustration of hurt-experienced and revenge-desired. If you look at all of David's life thus far, you will quickly realize that because of King Saul's great hatred of David, David lost everything that he really loved. In running from King Saul to save his own life, David had to leave his home, abandon his young new wife, forsake his friends, and even walk away from his job as a general in Israel's army. All of David's life was turned upside down by King Saul. Add to these losses the loneliness, exhaustion, fear, hunger and humiliation he experienced while on the run, and I'd say David had plenty of excellent reasons to seek vengeance. I don't think David was above fantasizing how he could get back at him; I'll just bet he thought of dozens of ways to kill King Saul, each one worse than the last. And I'll also bet he entertained those thoughts many times over. At the least, David must have absolutely longed for King Saul's death, if only for the freedom to get on with his own life.

How did David handle this desire and the opportunity for revenge?

No sooner had Jonathan given David the great encouraging words, "You will be King," than some men from the tribe of Ziphites ran directly to Saul to tell him that David was hiding among them. If it weren't for King Saul breaking off his pursuit of David in order to fight the Philistines, David might have been toast. But instead of getting caught, David was able to extract himself from an indefensible position in the desert and relocate his army to a place called En Gedi.

En Gedi was actually an oasis on the western shore of the Dead Sea and was known during that time as a great place to hole up because of the spring that provided a constant source of water. In addition, En Gedi had a sizable network of caves that threaded throughout the hills above the oasis. Being able to get his men into a well-hidden place with running water was probably a 'Whew!' moment for David and his men, but as things went on, the break in the action didn't last very long.

After pursuing the Philistines for a while, King Saul was once again informed of where David and his army were hiding. Scripture doesn't tell us whether or not King Saul even engaged the Philistines in a battle, so you get the idea that the moment he heard where David was, he immediately forgot about pursuing the Philistines. Obviously, finding David and killing him was the top priority. So, King Saul, rather than fighting the Philistines like he should have, chose 3,000 "especially skilled" soldiers and headed off to En Gedi in pursuit of David.

There are two things to note here. First, the soldiers that King Saul chose were not merely rag-tag foot soldiers—they were the elite of Israel's army. You could view them as the combination of our Green Berets and Navy Seals. Second, King Saul's 3,000 soldiers outmanned David's motley crew by about five to one. Both of these things testify to the fact that Saul was not messing around; he really wanted David dead.

Well, off King Saul and his elite army went, climbing the crags of the hills of En Gedi, poking their heads in every cave and checking out every nook and cranny looking for David. Suddenly King Saul felt nature calling. And yes, scripture really says this! So, thinking he'd get a little privacy, King Saul decided to go into the nearest cave to take care of business. What he didn't realize was that David and his men were hiding way in the back of that very cave. What a picture! Here was Saul, all by himself in a kind of physical position that would certainly not allow him to do much defensive sword play, with David just a few feet away.

This was too sweet! Oh, blessed revenge! To kill King Saul while he was relieving himself! The stories that could be told! The jokes that could be made! The king would not only lose his life, but would become the laughing stock of all of Israel! This was the opportunity of a life-time! Oh, David! Remember all of the humiliation, all of the running, all of the loss and hurt Saul has caused you? Come on, take your revenge!

Interestingly, sometime during his sojourn in that very cave while hiding from King Saul, David wrote a couple of Psalms, one of which is Psalm 142. I have to say, this is one of the most poignant Psalms David ever wrote. He said:

> *...no one is concerned for me. I have no refuge; no one cares for my life. I cry to you, "O LORD?" I say, "You are my refuge, my portion in the land of the living." Listen to my cry, for I am in desperate need; rescue me from those who pursue me, for they are too strong for me. Set me free from my prison, that I may praise your name* (Psalm 142:4-7).

Do you feel David's despair? His loneliness? His pain? Look at what he's experiencing here: He said, "I cry," and then asked the Lord to, "Listen to my cry." And what was he crying about? "I am in desperate need," because, "no one is concerned about me," "I have no refuge," and "no one cares for my life." You can easily determine from the words of this Psalm that David was at the end of his rope; he needed some kind of relief from the devastation of his life.

Now, wouldn't you think that having King Saul walk right into David's hidey-hole could actually be considered an answer to David's cry? Absolutely! Even all of David's soldiers were encouraging him to kill Saul. "This is the day," they said, "the Lord is giving the enemy into your hands."

David's response?

"God forbid I should do such a thing to my master, the Lord's anointed, or lift my hand against him; for he is the anointed of the Lord." With these words David rebuked his men and did not allow them to attack Saul (1 Samuel 24:6-7).

Can you believe this? It was the perfect circumstance for revenge, and David refused to kill his enemy! Instead, David got his knife out and silently crept up to King Saul. He deftly grabbed the king's robe and sliced off a big piece right at the corner. He then moved stealthily back to his men, waiting for King Saul to exit the cave.

David waited a few moments for Saul to get several paces away from the mouth of the cave. He then called down to Saul as he was scaling back down the hill to reunite with his army.

"Hey, Saul, my lord and King!"

King Saul immediately turned around to see David standing above him. When David saw him turn, David got down on his knees, and then prostrated himself on the ground before the king.

Then David stood up and cried, "Saul! Why do you listen to the people who tell you that I'm determined to kill you? You walked right into my cave, and I didn't lay a hand on you. Some of my soldier's urged me to kill you, but I told them that I couldn't do it because you are still God's anointed King. You don't believe me, Saul? Here, look at this piece of robe in my hand! This should prove to you that I am not guilty of any wrongdoing or rebellion against you. But while I've done nothing to harm you, you continue to hunt me down like a dog, trying to murder me."

Now here comes the most important part of David's speech which gives us the reason why he refused to take his revenge on King Saul:

> *May the Lord judge between you and me. And may the Lord avenge the wrongs you have done to me, but my hand will not touch you. As the old saying goes, "From evildoers come evil deeds," so my hand will not touch you* (1 Samuel 24:12-13).

Aha! "May the **Lord** judge…may the **Lord** avenge."

David refused to kill King Saul because of a few things he knew about God. Look at these two words: "judge" and "avenge." It was not a mistake that David used these two words together. Actually, "judge" is not merely an activity God does, but is rather an aspect of God's nature; God is a judge. "Judge" is part of who God is. "Avenge" (or better, "revenge"), on the other hand, is an action God takes as a result of His judgment.

What does this whole idea of God-as-judge mean?

In its broadest definition, "to judge" (*šāpat* in Hebrew) simply means to exercise the processes of government. But there are a couple of reasons why this simple definition does not describe everything involved in what David was asking God to do on his behalf.

The first reason is that when the word *šāpat* is translated as "judge" in the Bible, our modern minds immediately think about the judicial function of government that deals only with civil law. But remember we're talking here about an ancient Semitic people who did not differentiate between the secular and the sacred. In the ancient world, rendering judgment on something was not confined to just civil life. There were no limitations on what could be brought before the judge; judgment could be made on anything, extending itself to every part of one's life—civil, religious, and domestic.

There is a second reason to broaden the definition of "judge." While people living during the Old Testament times knew full well what laws were (Israel had the Ten Commandments, and the Babylonians had Hammurabi's Code of Laws), they never thought of themselves as a people ruled by laws alone. Rather, they were ruled by **the people** who dispensed the law. So, the law was never merely the function of one's government, but was rather centered **in a person**. This idea was so ingrained in the Semitic mind, that to this day, among the Arab tribes of the desert, judgments on every matter of life are not made by referring to a written code of law, but are made by the elders of the tribe who have the wisdom of experience and the trust of the people. This ensures their decisions will be respected as law by all in the tribe.

So let me clarify the idea of "judge" in scripture so we can understand what David was asking of God:

First, David was asking God to **act as ruler**. This is really important for David. Remember that the human ruler at the time was King Saul. Although he was the King, his ability to make judgment on anything was skewed, to say the least. So, David was asking God to be the King over the present King and the Lord over the present Lord. God alone can exercise the true ultimate rulership simply because He is God. All true authority is God's, and He shall ultimately act as judge of the world in the final judgment. Even King Saul himself ultimately bent his will to God's and accepted that He chose David to be king.

Second, because *šāpat* also means to decide cases of controversy as judge in civil, domestic and religious legal action, David was asking God to render **legal** judgment. David asked God to do this because God alone is wholly righteous—there is no way that God can render an unjust verdict; His judgment can never be skewed by personal deficiencies. Furthermore, God knows not only the facts of the case, but also the very hearts of the individuals who are involved in the case. God's knowledge goes beyond what the mouth says and sees the very intentions of the human heart. God knows the truth and can therefore render a righteous judgment.

Third, because **persons** rather than mere laws ruled the ancient world, the judge had both executive and judicial powers. That is, the judge also had the right and the power to carry out any judicial decisions. So, David made the statement to King Saul, "May the Lord be our judge (*šāpat*) and decide between us. May he consider my cause and uphold it, may he vindicate me by delivering me from your hand" (1 Samuel 24:15). In saying this, David's request for God to "vindicate" and "deliver" was based on the fact that God has the ability to judge righteously and carry out that righteous judgment. It is God's duty to vindicate and to deliver David because God is the Righteous Judge.

So, what does all of this have to do with revenge? Well, the lessons to be learned are: God is the ultimate ruler; God is Himself righteous and can therefore render righteous judgment; God has the duty to carry out His righteous judgment; and He alone has the ability to avenge those who have been misused and abused.

This whole idea of allowing God to avenge us becomes even more important when we understand what the act of "revenge" is all about. The concept of revenge, or vengeance, as understood by people during the time in which David lived, comes from the Hebrew word for "vengeance," *nāqam.* The first important thing to note about this word is that most of the uses of *nāqam* involve God as the source of vengeance. There's a classical passage using this word that's quoted quite a lot. Deuteronomy 32:35, 41 says, "'Vengeance is mine', says the Lord ... 'I will repay them who hate me.'" Wow! These are really strong words!

Honestly, I would much rather talk exclusively about God's love and mercy. But the truth is, God cannot be true to His own character of holiness and justice if He allows people who have abused others to go unpunished. In fact, as you read through some of the Old Testament, especially the Book of Isaiah, you will discover that Isaiah especially stressed "the day of the Lord's vengeance" as times in history when God sets the record straight. Lest we're tempted to say, "Well, since the coming of Jesus, it's a new day," this idea of God's vengeance is not only reserved for the Old Testament understanding of God, but is seen in the New Testament, as well. In the very last book of the Bible, John's Revelation, you will find that God, in the life to come, will "tread out the winepress" and "trample his enemies in his wrath."

You can't talk about God's wrath, however, without talking about God's mercy. The Bible always beautifully balances the fury of God's vengeance against the evildoer with the great majesty of His mercy. That is, God's vengeance can never be viewed apart from his great desire to show mercy. As one Bible commentary says, He is not *only* the God of wrath, but *must* be the God of wrath in order for His mercy to have meaning. So the focus of the Bible is not on God's vengeance being wreaked upon horrible people, but rather on God's mercy being freely given to those who trust in Him. God's way of doing things is always justice **plus** mercy.

Unfortunately, human beings do not have the capability to be perfect in justice and mercy, and this David knew very well. Killing King Saul would have only been an I-kill-you-before-you-kill-me kind of act. David was wise enough to know that this was no way to begin his rule as King of Israel. Once started down the road of murdering people who hated him, David would have had a difficult time knowing where to stop.

You see, a big part of the reason why only God should judge and avenge is because of the way wreaking revenge on someone affects us.

I have a great friend who was a missionary in a Central American country during a time when a grassroots revolution arose against the country's government, which was accused of being ultimately responsible for horrible injustices against its people. Mike told me that while the revolution started out as a peaceful movement, it soon became violent, with much of the country's civilian population bearing arms and fighting a war against the government's army. It's understandable how things easily turned violent due to the suppressed anger of the people who had been forced to live under a horrible oppression for years.

Well, Mike tells the story of a general in the revolution's army who, after several days of severe and bloody fighting, succeeded in taking control of a large village. The general led his rag-tag warriors into the center of the village and dispersed some of his soldiers into the town to find anyone who had colluded with the established and unjust government. It wasn't long before they found the mayor and his family. The general ordered his soldiers to drag the entire family out of their hiding place and lined them all up in the center of the town square. Without the benefit of legal trial or witnesses, he ordered them bound and gagged, and in front of the entire village of men, women and children, the general had them all shot dead on the spot.

The general then moved into the mayor's house, setting up his headquarters there. When he went back to the mayor's bedroom, he noticed several of the mayor's personal items left in plain sight. So, he slipped the mayor's Rolex over his own wrist, slid the mayor's sunglasses over his own eyes, and grabbed the mayor's car keys. The general walked outside and slid behind the wheel of the mayor's Mercedes. Mike said that as the general reached up to adjust the rear view mirror, he caught a glimpse of his own face. At that moment, Mike told me, something clicked in the general's mind. With great horror, he admitted to himself, "I have become the mayor."

You see, the major reason why taking revenge is harmful to us is because the act does nothing to rid us of the initial humiliation, or hurt. It does nothing to restore our sense of self-worth, but rather has the opposite effect. When we begin to use the same tactics on those who have hurt us in order to get revenge, we actually begin to turn into the person upon whom we have wreaked our revenge. On the other hand, if we allow God to do the avenging and the judging, a renewed sense of self will always occur.

After David finished his speech to Saul, scripture says this: *"Saul asked, 'Is that your voice, David my son?' And he wept aloud" (1 Samuel 24:16).*

Wow! These were not just crocodile tears that King Saul was shedding; this was his emotional admission that he had wronged David. "You are a better man than I," Saul said. "And while you have treated me well, I have treated you badly. The Lord actually delivered me into your hands, but you didn't kill me. May the Lord reward you well for the way you treated me today" (1 Samuel 24:17, 18).

Can you imagine? Unlike most leaders we know, the King is actually admitting wrongdoing. But here's the kicker. King Saul then said, "I know that you will surely be king and that the kingdom of Israel will be established in your hands" (1 Samuel 24:20).

Amazing! Not always, but sometimes, just like with Saul, when you allow God to avenge you, it may be that God will be able to bring that person to a place of repentance and regret for what he has done to you.

David ends Psalm 142 by appealing to God. He says, "Set me free from my prison, that I may praise your name. Then the righteous will gather about me because of your goodness to me" (Psalm 142:7). Isn't this an interesting way to end this Psalm of lament? What is the prison David is talking about? And, what does the righteous gathering around David have to do with David being set free from this prison?"

Let me suggest something.

Earlier in the Psalm, David had bemoaned that no one was concerned for him, and no one cared for his life (Psalm 142:4). Even though David was surrounded by his army, the hurt he had received from "Father" Saul was so deep, so damaging, so life-encompassing that David felt as if no one cared about him; that no one was concerned for him. This kind of response to hurt is absolutely debilitating. When someone has hurt us this deeply, our knee-jerk reaction is to isolate ourselves. Emotional walls go up all around us, built strong and high for the express purpose of protecting us from anyone who could possibly ever hurt us like this again. The trouble with building these kinds of walls is that while they may keep others out, they also very successfully keep us in, becoming a a kind of self-made prison. This is the prison to which David was referring.

David was smart enough to know, however, that getting revenge against the one who had hurt him so deeply would not release him from his prison of isolation from others. Rather, David understood that only God was able set him free from this kind of prison. And while David never did enjoy relationship with King Saul ever again, the righteous did gather around David, allowing him to enjoy wonderful and rich relationship for the rest of his life.

I promise you, when you allow God to be your avenger and judge rather than taking things into your own hands, you will always find a renewal of your sense of self-worth, honor and identity. And in the process, you will be freed from the prison of hurt and isolation, and enriched with deep and fruitful relationships with the righteous who will gather around you.

Works Cited

Beaumont, L. R. (2005-2009). *Revenge: Getting Even.* Retrieved November 10, 2009, from Emotional Competency: EmotionalCompetency.com

Chapter 6

WHEN I FORGET WHO I AM

1 Samuel 25 – Psalm 57

A friend told me the following story. When she was 15 years old her father asked her to come into his study to have a serious talk with him. She sat down in front of his desk, waiting expectantly to hear what her Dad had to say. Without any preliminary, he leaned over his desk and said, "Candace, you are a very plain girl. Because of that you probably won't get asked out on many dates. In fact, I really doubt that you'll ever get married. So," he continued, "since you'll most likely be living life alone, I suggest you really apply yourself to a good education so you'll be able to take care of yourself financially for the rest of your life."

Ouch. Actually, double ouch. You can only imagine what Candace began to think about herself—her entire life shifted with these few, damaging words. You can also imagine how quickly she would go from being a relatively happy teenage girl to feeling like she was so homely that no boy would ever want to be with her. Her very identity as a woman was wounded to the core.

What we're talking about here is a thing called self-identity—who we think we are. How important is this? Well, how we feel about ourselves affects virtually every aspect of our lives. In fact, Peter Burke and Jan Stets suggests that many of the successes and failures we experience in various areas of our lives are closely related to the ways that we have learned to view ourselves (Tangney, 2003). Here are a few thoughts about this whole issue of self-identity.

According to sociologists Jan Stets and Chris Biga, there are at least three things we need to realize about self-identity: it is learned, it is organized, and it is dynamic (Stets and Biga, 21).

Let's first address the idea that one's **self-concept is learned**. As far as we know, no one is born with a self-concept. Rather, it is thought that one's identity gradually emerges in the early months of life and is shaped and reshaped through repeated perceived experiences, particularly within the family unit. The simple fact that self-concept is learned has some important implications:

- Because our self-concept is developed through our experiences, there is almost unlimited potential for change in the way we perceive ourselves.
- Because of our life experiences and personal perceptions of those experiences, we may end up seeing ourselves differently than the way others see us.

- We tend to view different aspects of ourselves at different times with varying degrees of insight. So, new awareness of our identity can occur at any time.
- Any experience that we have that doesn't match up with our personal self-concept can be identified as a threat to our very personhood. The more we experience these "threats," the more we will attempt to protect ourselves in order to maintain our self-concept.

So, even though our self-identity is learned and has an amazing ability to change and grow, we actually have the ability to stop any growth or change in the way we view ourselves. This can happen when a new revelation about our self doesn't fit into our old mental grid. For example, it would be easy for my "plain" friend to become really flustered when she hears compliments about how she looks. Why? Because being pretty does not fit into her view about herself that was established by the voice of her dad saying, "You're plain, Candace, you're plain."

Second, **self-concept is organized**. Most researchers agree that self-concept has a generally stable quality that is characterized by orderliness and harmony. People will actually have many perceptions about themselves, but amazingly, all of these perceptions will coordinate with each other. It is this generally stable and organized quality of self-concept that gives consistency to one's personality. In fact:

- A healthy self-concept requires consistency, stability, strength, and tends to resist change. If self-concept changed readily, we would lack a consistent and dependable personality.
- The more central a particular belief is to our self-concept, the more resistant we are when it comes to changing that belief.
- At the heart of self-concept is the self-as-doer. We can actually obtain a sense of identity as a result of what we do.

- Because basic perceptions of our self are quite stable, any change that occurs in our self-identity takes time.
- Perceived successes and failures affect our self-concept. Perceived failure in a really important area of our life actually lowers the level of self-confidence in all other areas of life as well. Conversely, success in a prized area raises the level of self-confidence in other seemingly unrelated areas.

So, for example, if my "plain" friend went out on a series of dates with a guy that she really liked and respected, and received positive compliments about her appearance consistently and over a period of time, she would have a greater possibility of changing her self-identity. Simply, she would begin to hear a different voice saying entirely different things about her personal appearance.

Last, **self-concept is dynamic**. To understand the active nature of self-concept, it helps to imagine it as a compass: a continuously active system that dependably points to the "true north" of a person's perceived existence. This guidance system not only shapes the ways we view ourselves, others, and the world, but it also serves to direct our actions and enables us to take a consistent "stance" in life. Rather than viewing self-concept as the cause of behavior, it is better understood as the gyrocompass, the "true north" of human , providing consistency and direction for behavior. The following list describes the ways in which our self-concept is dynamic:

- The world and the things in it are not just perceived; they are always comprehended through the grid of our self-concept.
- Self-concept development is a continuous process. When we have a healthy personality, there is constant incorporation of new ideas and rejection of old ideas throughout life.
- We will always attempt to behave in ways that are in keeping with our self-concepts, no matter how helpful or hurtful to ourselves or to others.

- Self-concept usually takes precedence over the physical body. We will often sacrifice physical comfort and safety for emotional satisfaction.
- Self-concept continuously guards itself against loss of self-esteem, for it is this loss that produces feelings of anxiety.
- If self-concept must constantly defend itself from belittling words or actions from others, growth opportunities for a person's self-identity are severely limited.

Simply said, because her father's voice was such a strong voice in her experience, "plain" Candace will tend to perceive herself as a plain person for the rest of her life, no matter what other individuals say about her. In fact, she could even use this as an excuse to stop growing as an individual in **any area** of her life.

Let's face it: what we think about ourselves affects **everything**! It affects what we do, the choices we make, the way we perceive the world and those around us. If our perception of ourselves is skewed, everything else in our lives is going to be skewed.

So, the big question is, how in the world do we obtain a right and good self-identity? To whom do we go in order to hear the truth about who we are? Our dad, mom, husband, wife, friends, or kids? Well, not really. As close as these people may be to us, they still don't know the *real* us. There's only one person who knows us well enough to give us true self-identity, and that is the one who created us—God Himself. So how do we use God as our source of self-identity? Look at how it happened for David.

One day, God sent a man named Samuel to David's house to tell him, "God says you're the King." Was this merely a description of what

David would do with his life—a new occupation or a surprise undertaking? Absolutely not! "King" defined who David was as a person. "King" was David's true self-identity, given by God Himself. In fact, I could go so far as to say that "King" was the way God viewed David. And after all, this is God's desire—for us to view ourselves the way He views us.

This kind of self-identity changes everything! From the moment Samuel identified him as King, David made every decision and related to every person (including King Saul and the royal family!) just like the king he truly was. Even though he had yet to sit on the throne in Jerusalem, his God-given self-identity ("King") was at the very core of David's being.

But, as we all know, when life happens it's sometimes hard to remember who we are. The horrifying thing about those times in life is that if we are not reminded of our true identity, we can really mess things up. This is what happened in David's life.

After King Saul's important declaration that David would, indeed, become King (1 Samuel 24:20), Saul returned home from En Gedi to Gibeah. Even though it looked like he was going to stop chasing him, David still did not trust the king in the least—so he and his men stayed in their stronghold in the hills.

The very next portion of scripture contains some really bad news for David. It simply says, "Now Samuel died." Samuel was, of course, the prophet of God who anointed young David as King; but as importantly, Samuel was to be one of David's staunchest supporters and most loyal of friends throughout his sojourn in the desert. Obviously, this was distressing news for David. Not only did he lose a friend, but he lost the prophet who served as a constant reminder that God had chosen him to be king. And King he would become. It was of ultimate importance for David to remember that his movement toward the fulfillment of God's promise was not born of a human lust for power, or even a dream for personal greatness; it was instead a God-ordained reality. Samuel's presence in David's life served as a constant reminder of who David truly was. And even though the promise had yet to come to fruition, David **was** the anointed King of Israel.

Samuel's death was not a personal loss for David alone; but scripture says that all of Israel mourned, with thousands attending the burial in his hometown of Ramah. Certainly a light had gone out in Israel.

After Samuel's funeral, David and his army moved into the hill country of Judah into a place called Carmel. The name "Carmel" actually means "vineyard land" or better, "the garden spot." Evidently, this region was a very beautiful and agriculturally productive part of the country.

Living in that area was a wealthy man named Nabal and his wife, Abigail. Abigail is described as being both intelligent and beautiful, a winning combination in any woman! But Nabal, on the other hand, was the total opposite of his wife; he was surly and mean. Interestingly, even the names of this couple speak to their personalities. In Hebrew, the name *Abigail* means "my Heavenly Father is joy," while *Nabal* simply means "fool."

After hearing that Nabal was busy shearing his flock of 3,000 sheep, David decided to send ten young men ahead to greet Nabal in his name. David's message to Nabal through his men was: "Good health to you, Nabal, and your entire household! And good health to all that is yours! I hear that this is sheep-shearing day for you, the day of great joy and feasting, and I want to remind you that while we have been in and around this area for several months, no harm ever came to your shepherds or your sheep. In fact, we worked hard to protect all that you have from harm. So as a courtesy, please allow us to join you in your feasting. Just give us anything you can find for us to eat."

After faithfully relaying David's message, the ten men waited for Nabal's reply.

"Who is this David?" Nabal bellowed. "Who is this son of Jesse... Why should I take my bread and water, and the meat I have slaughtered for my shearers and give it to men coming from who knows where?"

OK, now this was not good. Not only was he turning away visitors from his table—a huge taboo among the tribes in the East—but he was unwilling to share even a little bread and water, the most minor of sustenance, with David and his men. No wonder Nabal's name means "foolish!"

On that note, David's men turned around, returned to the group, and reported every word that Nabal had said. David had a four-word response: "Put on your swords." And with that, David and 400 of his men went to meet Nabal.

Now, one of Nabal's servants who had overheard the exchange between his master and David's men ran immediately to Nabal's wife, Abigail. "David sent messengers from the desert to give our master his greetings," he said, "but he hurled insults at them. Yet, mistress, these men were very good to us. They didn't mistreat us; they didn't steal from us. In fact, night and day they were like a wall of protection around us and our flocks. Please think quickly," he pled, "because disaster is about to come down on our heads. You know the master will do nothing. He is such a wicked man that no one can talk to him."

Abigail didn't waste a minute. She ran to the kitchens and gathered up the food that had been prepared for the feast and loaded it all on donkeys. You can't really appreciate how massive the undertaking was unless you understand the logistics. Here's the menu:

- 200 loaves of bread
- Two skins of wine
- Five dressed sheep
- Five bushels of roasted grain
- 100 raisin cakes, and
- 200 fig cakes

OK, that should about feed an army! And Abigail accomplished all of this without Nabal finding out what she was doing.

She sent the servants on ahead with the food and followed behind on her own donkey. Just as David and his men were coming down a ravine, she intercepted them. David had just been saying to the men around him, "It's been useless—all my watching over the guy's property in the desert! He has paid me back evil for good. May God himself deal with me," David said, "if by morning I leave alive one male of all who belong to this man's household!"

Wait a minute! Was this the same David who had just refused to kill his arch enemy, King Saul? You mean to tell me that David was getting ready to kill the entire male population of a household over an insult, yet refused to lift a hand against giving us all of the gory details of the man who made multiple attempts to murder him? What's going on here?

Overhearing what David had just said, Abigail jumped off her donkey, fell at David's feet and bowed down before him with her face to the ground. "My lord," she said to David. "Let the blame for this insult be on me alone. Give me a chance to tell you what has happened." Still on her knees, Abigail pleaded, "Please don't pay any attention to my husband. Please don't take what he said to you seriously. He's always making trouble; after all, his name is Nabal, and he acts just like his name—a Fool—and folly always follows him."

"Now, master," Abigail said to David, "up to this point the Lord has kept you from avenging yourself with your own hands. Don't let any wrongdoing be found in you as long as you live. Please forgive Nabal's offense to you, for the Lord will certainly make a lasting dynasty for you because you fight the Lord's battles, not your own. When the Lord has done for you every good thing he promised and has appointed you king over Israel, you will not have on your conscience the staggering burden of needless bloodshed or of having avenged yourself simply because you refused to forgive a fool. And let me tell you something else: even though someone is pursuing you in order to kill you, your life will be bound securely in the bundle of the living by the Lord your God. But the lives of your enemies God will hurl away as from the pocket of a sling" (1 Samuel 25:29).

By not killing King Saul, David had proved himself to be a man who was not interested in revenge—an unlikely trait for a king. But now, frustrated and angry over a fool's actions, David wanted more than anything to make Nabal and his household pay…, and pay dearly. But this would not be the action of a king—David had forgotten who he truly was.

While Abigail had fallen on her face in honor of David's position as anointed King, she did not grovel nor beg David for mercy. Rather, she reminded David of who he was. "The Lord will certainly make a lasting dynasty for you…when he has appointed you king over Israel," Abigail said. And to further underscore David's identity, she added that God would hurl away David's enemies "as from the pocket of a sling." This was simply Abigail's way of saying to David, "Don't you remember the day you killed Goliath with your sling? Don't you remember how God anointed you as King over Israel, then confirmed that by empowering you to sling a small stone that felled a giant? Remember who you are, David! You're God's anointed King—act like it!"

David's response? "Praise God!" he declared. "He sent you to meet me! And praise be to your good sense! Bless you for keeping me from murder and taking things into my own hands! As God lives, if you had not come as quickly as you did, stopping me in my tracks, by morning there would have been nothing left of Nabal and all the men in your household." Then David accepted the food that Abigail had brought and said, "Return home in peace. I've heard what you've said and will do what you have asked (1 Samuel 25:30).

Disaster for David was avoided, simply because he was clearly reminded of who he really was. After this, David and his men were back in

...ice again hiding from King Saul. It was here that David wrote

> Have mercy on me, O God, have mercy on me, for in you my
> soul takes refuge. I will take refuge in the shadow of your
> wings until the disaster has passed.
> I cry out to God Most High, to God who fulfills his purpose for
> me. He sends from heaven and saves me, rebuking those who
> hotly pursue me...

Look at how closely David's prayer reflects what Abigail had told him that day in the lush land near Carmel:

Abigail said to David:	David said to God:
Your life will be bound securely in the bundle of the living by the Lord your God	*In you my soul takes refuge. I will take refuge in the shadow of your wings.*
The lives of your enemies God will hurl away as from the pocket of a sling	*He sends from heaven and saves me rebuking those who hotly pursue me*
Lord will certainly make a lasting dynasty for you; and [will] appoint[ed] you king over Israel	*God...fulfills his purpose for me*

Something really amazing happens when we are reminded who we are; we also remember who God is.

Esther Ntoto is a beautiful Congolese woman who works with female victims of her country's civil war. She keeps me informed of the atrocities that continue to occur in the Republic of Congo. Not only have nearly 4-million people died since the civil war began there in 1998, but nearly one in three women in that country have been brutally raped by armed soldiers. It is not enough that most of these soldiers have passed on AIDS to these women, or even that they leave many of them pregnant with HIV-positive children, but the violence of the rape leaves many women with a physical condition called fistula—a rupturing of the walls that separate the vagina from the bladder or rectum. This condition causes incontinence of the worst kind and, according to Esther, requires several surgeries in order to be repaired.

Because of the social structure of the Congolese people, these women are cast out of their families with no hope of living a normal life as a married woman. Nor can many of them ever have children because of the violence done to their bodies. I suppose most horrifying of all is that in the hospital where Esther ministers, she has seen girls as young as six months and women as old as 86 years old brought in to the hospital needing multiple surgeries to repair their fistula. The horror that these soldiers perpetrate upon these women is indescribable, especially in light of the fact that we believe God created humanity in His own image.

After listening to Esther's experiences with these women, I confess that my attitude toward these Congolese soldiers was way less than godly, and waxed quite eloquently about my position on the whole issue. Esther sadly smiled at me and said, "Yes, Sheri, it is horrible what they do to women. But equally as horrible is what is being done to create this kind of soldier. You see," she continued, " the army's leaders will go into a village and kidnap the boys living there, many of them as young as seven or eight years old, and put them through horrible torture in order to turn these young boys into violent and hateful soldiers. So these boy-soldiers are really victims of violence perpetuating violence on others."

Then, Esther got practical with me. "If you really want to understand what's going on in my country," she said, "watch the movie *Blood Diamond.*"

Acted out in horribly visual detail, the film *Blood Diamond,* tells the story of civil war occurring in Sierra Leone, with rebel soldiers conscripting young boys to fight the war and work in diamond mines. The products of these mines have come to be known as "conflict diamonds," with the proceeds of the diamond sales being used to bankroll rebel activity. Caught up in the conflict is Solomon Vandy, a fisherman from the Mende tribe, who was conscripted by the rebels to work in a diamond mine, and his young son, Dia, who had been kidnapped and brainwashed by the rebel army.

While working in the mine, Solomon discovered a large pink diamond worth millions of dollars. He recognized it as a ticket out of Sierra Leone for him and his family—if only he could successfully keep his diamond hidden from the rebels and sell it himself.

Not long after, Solomon met diamond broker Danny Archer, and they came up with a plan to rescue Dia from the rebel forces and, at the same time, recover the priceless diamond. They rescued Dia from the rebels and killed a few government soldiers in the process. After this, Archer and Dia stood at the site of the hidden diamond, taking watch while Solomon furiously dug.

Standing behind Solomon, Archer whispered anxiously, "Keep digging, huh? Soldiers will be here any second. It had better be there, huh?"

"Yes, yes," Solomon replied.

"Have you got it?"

Solomon picked the diamond out of the hole. "Yes, got it. Oh, yes." He began to unroll the diamond from its burlap cocoon and looked up with great hope in his eyes only to see his son pointing a gun at him. The rebels had so brainwashed Dia that even though now free, he continued to look at his father as a traitor to the rebel cause.

"Dia, what are you doing?" Solomon asked. "Look at me. What are you doing? You are Dia Vandy. Of the proud Mende tribe." Yet Dia continued to point the gun at his father. "You are a good boy who loves soccer and school."

Solomon walked nearer to Dia with tears streaming down his face. "Your mother loves you so much. She waits by the fire making plantains and red palm oil stew with your sister N'Yanda and the new baby." His voice broke as he said, "The cows wait for you. And Babu, the wild dog who minds no one but you."

As long-repressed memories of his home and family came flooding back, Dia began to weep. "I know they made you do bad things, but you are not a bad boy," Solomon assured him. "I am your father who loves you. And you will come home with me and be my son again."

Who are you? Does your self-identity line up with who your Heavenly Father says you are? Or, have you been listening to the negative voices in your past that have told you, "You're plain," "You're too fat," "You're stupid" or "You'll never amount to anything." Have you allowed those voices to define you?

Candace sure didn't.

As Candace grew up, she began to hear a different view of who she was from people around her. Even at that, it took a while for Candace to ask herself a really important question: "Is what my father said about me actually true?" And, after the question took root, it even took a while longer for Candace to realize that her father had psychological difficulties that drove him to make Candace feel small and insignificant; problems that a 15-year-old young woman was certainly not equipped to recognize.

So what did Candace do when she realized that her father had actually told her a lie about who she was?

She went to Father God who told her only the truth about who she was; beautiful and beloved. Not only was Candace then free to hear what God said about her, her true identity was confirmed over and over by those friends around her, both men and women, whose opinion she could really trust.

In reality, Candace **is anything** but plain. She's always been anything but plain. But it required her to open herself to God's word of truth about her identity to set her free to become all that God had in mind for her.

It is supremely important to God that you hear from him the truth about who you are! Let me remind you that even after David's major supporter and constant reminder of his identity, Samuel, died, God sent another supporter and reminder-of-identity into David's life in the person of Abigail.

I ask again, who are you? Choose to listen to the voice of the God who created you, knows you better than anyone, and continues to transform you into His image. Hear Him tell you who you really are. Knowing and living in accordance with the person who God says you are changes everything!

Works Cited

Biga, J. E. (21). Bringing Identity Theory into Environmental Sociology. *Sociological Theory* , 398-423.

Tangney, M. R. (2003). A Sociological Approach to Self and Identity. In J. E. Burke, *Handbook of Self and Identity* (pp. 128-152). New York: The Guilford Press.

William G. Braude, T. (1987). *The Midrash on Psalms (Volume Two)*. New Haven: Yale University Press.

Williams, J. G. (1971). *Ten Words of Freedom: An Introduction to the Faith of Israel.* Minneapolis: Fortress Press.

WHEN I GET WHAT I THOUGHT I WANTED

2 Samuel 11/Psalm 51

W hen I was in my late teens, I was asked out on a date by the hunk of the year, the man of the moment, the Brad Pitt of the sixties, the guy who every girl wanted. I was totally incredulous. Me? He wanted ME to go out with him?

I spent all day getting ready for the big first date. When he arrived at my door to pick me up I was as beautiful as I was ever going to be—save for emergency plastic surgery, I had done all that could be done. As I slid into the passenger side of the car, my mantra began: "Stay cool. Stay cool. Stay cool."

Something must have worked, because before saying goodnight, Steve asked me out again. And again. And again. It wasn't long before I felt myself falling in love with him. There were so many things going for us. He was a preacher's kid; so was I. He felt a real call to ministry; so did I. Steve's mom thought I was wonderful; my parents loved him. So it seemed only natural that a few months later we announced our engagement.

As time went on, however, things began to happen that just didn't jibe with my starry-eyed perception of Steve. There were times, for example, when I would notice money missing from my wallet. There were nights when he'd say he was with certain friends, but when I tried to phone him at their apartment, he wouldn't be there. He'd tell me about conversations with people that had really ticked him off, but when I saw those people and referred to the conversations, they either didn't happen at all or were greatly exaggerated. Honestly, my internal alarm system was blaring at me, but I was a girl in love—I wanted him, so I totally ignored the warning signs.

About this time, my parents tried to talk to me. They were getting strange vibes from Steve and were afraid that continuing the relationship would be a huge mistake. I didn't listen to them. Some of my best friends, even a married couple in the church, talked to me about inconsistencies in Steve's life. I didn't listen to them either. Worse yet, God was talking to me about Steve, and I'm embarrassed to admit that I didn't listen to Him either. Good or bad, I wanted what I wanted, and I wanted Steve.

It's human nature, isn't it? There are some times we want something so badly, it doesn't matter whether or not the getting is good for us, or even if there are horrible ramifications. Many times we are so bent on satisfying our cravings that the loss of other relationships, our moral integrity, and our sense of well-being are nothing in comparison to that momentary feeling of joy when we get what we thought we wanted.

The best example of this kind of person in the Old Testament is a person who already had everything he could possibly want. King David, the darling of Israel and the apple of God's eye, was a good king as far as kings go, but he had terrible difficulties being a good man. Maybe all that time he spent in the desert running from King Saul gave him a skewed sense of reality. Or, it could have been that once David finally became King of Israel, his position of power gave him a feeling of entitlement that was not appropriate for God's chosen King.

For whatever reason, by the time we get to 2 Samuel 11 and 12, King David was at his worst. This is a familiar story to almost everyone; it's the story of David and Bathsheba. It's the story of a guy in a position of great power who took what he wanted and then had to live with the ramifications of his actions. At the same time, it's a story of God's great love and His ability to forgive the most heinous of sins.

Our story opens with Israel, once again, fighting a war against their notorious enemy the Ammonites. 2 Samuel 11:1 says that it was springtime, "When kings go off to war." (Because it was a strongly agrarian society in those days, there was actually a season for war squeezed in between planting and harvesting the fields). The emphasis is not on springtime, but rather the fact that the King always accompanied his men in battle. In this circumstance, however, King David decided to sit the war out, sending instead his second in command, Joab, with his special guard, and all of Israel's soldiers to lead the fight against the Ammonites.

David's first mistake? Neglecting a major responsibility as King of Israel: going to war with the rest of his men. Staying home in such situations was not King David's usual practice, of course. In fact, leading his troops into battle was the major external activity of an ancient Near Eastern ruler. Although reprehensible in itself, David's conduct on this occasion paved the way for royal behavior that was more despicable still.

David's second mistake? If he was going to skip the war, he should at least have been busy running the kingdom. But, no. Second Samuel chapter eleven tells us that, unable to sleep (probably due to lack of hard work and exercise!), King David found himself walking around the roof of the palace. From that vantage point he spotted a beautiful woman bathing. Lest David be labeled as a Peeping Tom along with his other foibles, it was very common in that day for individuals to bathe outside after the sun had set and the cool evening breeze kicked up, especially during the hot summer months. Granted, the King did have a particularly good vantage point from the much higher roof of his palace.

Well, his 'just looking' quickly turned into 'really wanting.' What makes the King's act especially despicable is that David knew who the woman was. She was Bathsheba, the wife of a man well known to him. In fact, Uriah, Bathsheba's husband, was not simply a soldier in the King's army, but was one of David's "Thirty Mighty Men"—probably a member of Jerusalem's nobility. Uriah was a man who was in close relationship with King David!

Things between the King and Bathsheba developed quickly. Notice how tersely the narrative continues in chapter eleven:

> *Then David sent messengers to get her. She came to him, and he slept with her. (She had purified herself from her uncleanness.) Then she went back home. The woman conceived and sent word to David, saying, "I am pregnant"* (2 Samuel 11:4-5).

I'm not sure that there was any collusion in this act on Bathsheba's part, but I will say that David certainly used his power as King to get exactly what he thought he wanted. And, it didn't seem to matter to him that Bathsheba was married to one of his close friends. Let's just say this was not one of the sterling moments in David's life. In spite of everything, he wanted Bathsheba, and he got Bathsheba—impregnating her in the process. The writer of 2 Samuel clarified that King David really was the father of the baby by including the parenthetical phrase "she had purified herself from her uncleanness" (2 Samuel 11:4), or (according to *The Message* version of the passage) "This occurred during the time of 'purification' following her period." Not one single doubt—this was the King's child. David got what he thought he wanted in Bathsheba, but now what?

Well, King David was no dummy. He knew that if his adulterous action and Bathsheba's pregnancy became public, it would totally ruin his reputation as God's anointed King. So, the great cover-up began. The first thing King David did was to send word to General Joab, asking that Bathsheba's husband, Uriah, be sent home from the war. You already know what David was planning, don't you? Yep, just have Uriah spend the night with his wife and no one would ever know that the child born was, in truth, the King's child.

David left nothing to chance. When Uriah returned home, King David invited him to the palace, where they sat and talked. Of course, the goal was to plant the idea in Uriah's head that he needed to go home to spend the night with his Bathsheba. The King was going to be cool, though…very cool. You can imagine the conversation…

"So, how's the war going?" King David asked.

"God is on our side," replied Uriah. "You should have been there. We besieged the capitol city, Rabbah, and many Ammonites have been killed."

"Good, good," said the King. "And how is Joab?"

"Joab's doing well, oh King. He's a great commander. Well, not as great as you, King David, but he's really good," Uriah said.

"And the soldiers," David asked, "how are they faring?"

"Well, it's war, King David. Many have died, and many more are wounded. The rations are running low, and we're all really tired. Say, is there a reason for bringing me home? Have I not done well? Have I not fought to the best of my ability? Have I offended you in some way?"

"Absolutely not," replied the King. "In fact, I brought you home as a kind of reward for the great job you're doing. Tell you what. Why don't you go down to your house and relax. I'll send dinner to you from my own table so that you and your wife can have an enjoyable evening."

David wasn't King for nothing. Could he play the game, or what?!

Only problem was that Uriah was much more loyal to Israel than King David had anticipated. Word came to the King the next morning that Uriah did not go home to spend the night with his wife, but rather slept with the servants at the entrance to the palace. When David asked him why in the world he didn't go home, Uriah said, "The ark and Israel and Judah are staying in tents and my master, Joab, and my lord's men are camped in the open fields. How could I go to my house to eat and drink and lie with my wife? As surely as you live, I will not do such a thing!" (2 Samuel 11:11).

Boy, even best laid plans can be upset! What did King David do? He asked Uriah to spend a couple more days in town to eat and drink with him. OK, this was somewhat twisted. How devious could he be? The King had now spent three days making nice with the husband of the woman he'd slept with. He even went so far as to get Uriah soused one night, but still Uriah slept on the king's mat among the servants rather than going home. It's impossible for us not to compare Uriah's integrity with the integrity of the king here. Uriah was completely loyal and true in his commitment to both the king and to Israel, while David, Israel's icon of what it meant to be God's man, had become a liar, a cheat, and soon, a murderer.

No matter how King David attempted to cover up his actions, the problem just would not go away! It seemed he only had one option left— kill Uriah and marry Bathsheba. That way, at least it would look like the baby was legitimately conceived. So, the King wrote a letter to Joab and gave it to Uriah to carry back with him to war. David wrote, "Put Uriah in the front line where the fighting is fiercest. Then withdraw from him so he will be struck down and die." How despicable! Uriah was actually carrying his own death warrant in his hand!

Well, it happened just as King David wanted. Joab stuck Uriah on the front lines of the battle, and sure enough, Uriah was killed. After Bathsheba went through the customary period of mourning—about seven days—the King married her.

End of story. Case closed. Mission accomplished.

Well, not quite. In prelude to what is to happen next, we have the sentence, "But the thing David had done displeased the Lord" (2 Samuel 11:27). Lust, adultery, lying, murder. You know that God wasn't about to let this go. Just when King David thought the cover-up had been successful, one of God's prophets, Nathan, showed up in open court.

Standing before the King, Nathan told this story:

There were two men in a certain town, one rich and the other poor. The rich man had a very large number of sheep and cattle, but the poor man had nothing except for one little female lamb. He raised it, and it grew up with him and his children. It shared his food, drank from his cup and even slept in his arms. The little lamb was like a daughter to him. He probably even named the lamb Fluffy.

Well, a traveler came to visit the rich man around dinnertime, but the rich man refused to take one of his own sheep or cattle to prepare a meal for the traveler. Instead, he crept into the yard of the poor man, stole Fluffy, and cooked her for his visitor.

"What," Nathan asked the King, "should be done to the wealthy thief?"

Without a pause and burning with anger, King David responded, "That evil man deserves death!" Likewise, without hesitation, Nathan declared in a loud voice, "You, O King, are the man!"(2 Samuel 12:7).

Can you even imagine? Open court in those days was equivalent to a live news broadcast on CNN or ABC. People would come from all over the Kingdom, crowding into the judgment hall to be entertained by the proceedings. And while Nathan's story centered on sheep, you can bet on the fact that everyone in King David's court—from the lowest servant to the most intimate of his royal counselors—knew what Nathan was really talking about. This was the ultimate example of having your dirty laundry hung out for everyone to see!

Let's face it; human beings simply don't like to be told "No." We want what we want, when we want it. So, King David got what he wanted. In addition, he also got a few things he didn't want: the ramifications that go along with such behavior. In King David's case, his actions were made public causing him to lose face among his own people and, as time went on, even his enemies. So not only did the King have to live with the memory of all of these terrible deeds, he now had tons of people to constantly remind him of every gory detail. And the great shame of it is that after all of David's maneuvering, the baby boy that Bathsheba gave birth to died within his first few days of life, making all of King David's manipulative acts inconsequential. Simply, a terrible end to a terrible story.

David got what he wanted, but it was not what God wanted for him. Read what Nathan told King David that God wanted for him:

> *This is what the LORD, the God of Israel, says: 'I anointed you king over Israel, and I delivered you from the hand of Saul. I*

*gave your master's house to you, and your master's wives into
your arms. I gave you the house of Israel and Judah. And if all
this had been too little,* **I would have given you even more.**
*Why did you despise the word of the LORD by doing what is
evil in his eyes?* (2 Samuel 12:7-9).

When will we ever learn that what God wants for us is so much
more amazing, more magnificent, and more glorious than what we think we
want for ourselves?

Not only did getting what he wanted instead of what God wanted
for him cause David to live life far below the level of fulfillment and joy that
God had planned for him, in the act of getting what he wanted, David
ended up doing "what was evil" in God's eyes. According to Jewish law,
these kinds of actions always have harsh repercussions. In David's case, the
sentence was death.

You've got to hand it to David, however. Before Nathan could even
take another breath, David responded, "I have sinned against the Lord" (2
Samuel 12:13).

Nathan then replied, "The Lord has taken away your sin. You are
not going to die" (2 Samuel 12:13-14). Wow! How amazing it is that God
not only has the capacity to "take away sin," but also reverse his judgment
of death when the guilty person repents!

David wrote about this whole situation in Psalm 51:

*Have mercy on me, O God, according to your unfailing love;
according to your great compassion blot out my transgressions.
Wash away all my iniquity and cleanse me from my sin.
For I know my transgressions, and my sin is always before me...
Create in me a pure heart, O God, and renew a steadfast spirit
within me...*

You do not delight in sacrifice, or I would bring it;
The sacrifices of God are a broken spirit; a broken and contrite
heart, O God, you will not despise
(Psalm 51:1-3l, 10, 16-17).

Notice that King David addressed the sin issue first. Yes, sin. Sometimes in the process of getting what we want, we have the ability to commit horrible sins. The obvious sins committed by David are of course, adultery and murder. However, if we replay the tape a bit, many other transgressions can be named: sexual lust for Bathsheba, coveting the wife of another man, lying in order to cover the act, and on and on. When King David referred to his transgressions in the plural, rest assured he had a passel of them.

When in this situation, to what did the King appeal for forgiveness? His own goodness? His rights as King? Hardly. David instead appealed to God's "unfailing love." This short phrase is actually made up of only one word in the Hebrew language. It is the word *hèsed*. This word is used numerous times in the Old Testament, 280 times to be exact, and can otherwise be translated as "mercy," or in the case of Psalm 51, "unfailing love." *Hèsed* is a powerful word, derived from the concept of a covenantal relationship. David was extremely savvy to utilize God's unfailing love in his prayer of repentance!

This idea of God's unfailing love within the bonds of covenant began early in the history of Israel. With the simple phrase, "I will be your God and you will be my people" found in Exodus 6:7, God chose Israel to be His own people. While a covenant is really a relationship between people with standards of commitment involved, the covenant that God has with His people is unilateral. That is to say, only God has the right to choose with whom He wants a relationship; only God has the right to make the rules or amend the rules of a successful relationship. The relationship God established with Israel was sealed with an agreement—a covenant. At the heart of His "rules of successful relationship" were the Ten Commandments or "God's ten words of freedom," as Old Testament scholar Jay G. Williams refers to them (Williams, 1971). As long as Israel held to the stipulations of relationship with God, great blessing and joy would be the result. If Israel disobeyed the stipulations, however, chaos in relationship would soon result, both with God and with one another.

Think about it. The Israelites were a nomadic people who spent forty years wandering in the desert in order to find the Promised Land. During this time, the people lived within the bounds of their own tribes, and later within the bounds of their own families. Can you even imagine the kind of chaos that would result if stipulations against murder or adultery or lying were not obeyed in this close-knit culture? Without obedience to God's stipulations of relationship, I doubt there would be a person left alive to enter the Promised Land!

But Israel was not the only participant that was required to stick to the rules of the covenant. God, too, was bound by his own laws. And this is where the concept of *hèsed* comes in. *Hèsed* is the word that is used to describe the element that binds individuals to one another and to God within the ties of covenant. This foundational element is understood in two ways:

First, *hèsed* is understood as God's loyalty to his covenant obligations, a loyalty that the Israelites should also practice in their relationship with God and with one another. Whether or not Israel obeyed the stipulations of the covenant, God—because He is God—was always loyal to his people. This means that when we've really messed up, God will loyally stand beside us, even when no one else will.

The second idea behind the word, *hèsed,* is the idea of God's love. It does not follow that God's love is merely one factor in a covenant; rather the covenant is the sign and expression of God's love for us. By way of illustration, take a look at how God begins the giving of his commandments to Moses:

> And [God] passed in front of Moses, proclaiming, "The Lord, the Lord the compassionate and gracious God, slow to anger, abounding in love (hèsed) and faithfulness, maintaining love (hèsed) to thousands, and forgiving wickedness, rebellion and sin (Exodus 34:6-7).

It is really important to note that God's love in the passage is described by two qualifiers: "abounding" and "maintaining," or clearer, longsuffering. How important are these qualifiers?

If you remember, King David had committed heinous sins. He murdered an innocent man, committed adultery in spite of his many wives and many more concubines, and lied so many times that he probably had a great deal of trouble remembering where to pick up the conversation. He got what he thought he wanted and flagrantly broke multiple stipulations of God's covenant in the process. So, to what does David appeal in Psalm 51 to get him out of the mess he's made? God's *hèsed*. God's loyal, unfailing, abounding, longsuffering love for people. David appealed for mercy on the basis of God's willingly assumed and continued obligation (His "loyal-love") to remove anything—including guilt—which threatens the welfare of anyone for whom He is responsible. Remember, David was merely human and has no power to command such mercy, but he could ask for it on the basis of his confession of sin and the prayer which followed David's request in Psalm 51.

Look at the phrases David used to describe his desire for God's acts of unfailing love: "blot out my transgressions," "wash away all my iniquity," "cleanse me from my sin." The three verbs used here are very significant!

The word "blot" literally means "to obliterate" or "to erase." This is a picture of God standing in front of a whiteboard on which our sins are listed one by one. David was asking God to get out his eraser and wipe the whiteboard clean.

The verb "wash" was meant to describe the act of washing clothes. If you've ever washed anything at all you know that you've got to have a cleansing agent and a lot of agitation. In order to clean clothing (pre-washing machine era) you'd need to get elbow deep in soapy water and provide your own agitation. What was David asking for? For God to get "elbow deep" in the dirtiest part of his life; to enter into the areas of secrecy and shadow, where David had attempted to hide his sin, and thoroughly wash those areas clean.

The last desire David had was for God to "cleanse" him. This word describes a ritual cleansing—a forensic cleansing. Here, David was not asking God to merely cleanse him from his sins, but rather David was crying out to God, "Cleanse ME!" This was David praying, "Oh, God, don't just clear away the acts of sin, but clean the thought of sin, the inclination toward sin...cleanse ME!"

But, are sins like murder and adultery too much for God to forgive? I mean, isn't there a limit to what God is willing to cleanse from the fabric of our lives?

I had come home early from work late one afternoon and flipped the television on to what I thought was the news. Instead, I saw the face of a well-known journalist, who leaned toward the sensational, interviewing a young man in prison garb. I quickly discovered that the young man was Sean Sellers, a teenaged Satanist awaiting execution for the murder of three people (two of whom were his mother and step-father), all the result of a Satanic ritual. As the journalist began asking questions about how in the world this young man found himself sitting on death row, Sellers' story began to unfold.

He gave his life over to darkness because he believed that Satan was, in his own words, "the force behind rebellion which led to freedom and was a way to success in a society where only the strong survive and only the ruthless attain the American dream." So to get what he wanted, Sean made a pact with Satan. In his own blood he wrote "I renounce God, I renounce Christ. I will serve only Satan. To my friends love, to my enemies death...

hail Satan" and signed his name at the bottom. He mutilated Bibles: burned them, urinated on them, and poured blood on them.

One night, after a lust ritual with a satanic priest, Sellers and a friend walked into a convenience store manned by a clerk who had insulted his friend's girlfriend and refused to sell them beer. Sellers pointed a .357 magnum pistol at the man and pulled the trigger. The first shot missed, the second shot wounded, and the third shot killed the man. The two boys walked out of the store taking no money and no merchandise, laughing with evil delight at the murder they had committed for Satan.

Several days later, Sellers took his step-father's .44 revolver and shot both of his parents in the head as they slept. He said, "I stood in front of my mother's convulsing body watching blood pour from a hole in her face, and laughed a hideous giggle. I had felt relieved, as if the world's oppression and been lifted from my shoulders."

It was at that point that the journalist leaned over the interview table and just below the level of a yell, incredulously asked, "How in the world can you live with yourself?"

I watched Sellers drop his head for a moment. When he raised it back up, tears were flowing down his cheeks. He choked out, "If it wasn't for the blood of Jesus, I wouldn't be able to live with myself."

If there ever was a guy that I thought was beyond the forgiveness of God, it would have been Sean Sellers. Satanist and murderer. Yet, God is so loyal, so abundant in his love, that He can even forgive a guy like Sean Sellers.

In his own testimony, Sellers said that two days after he was caught by the police, a man in the next cell handed him a paperback Bible. Sean said:

> *As I opened the paperback book and read from Psalms, an overwhelming sense of guilt fell upon me. I had been wrong. Satan had lied to me. It was God, not Satan, who only loved me...I had knelt at an altar of Satan covered in blood, full of hate toward the Creator. And still, my God loved me...for the first time I prayed, 'Lord, here I am again. If you will take me back I will serve you.' God touched me, honoring that prayer, and I began to cry...I had been forgiven and given an incomprehensible peace. At that moment, I knew true love and realized all I had sought all along was only this, and finally I was free.*

The moral of the story? Actually, Sean Sellers **did** get what he wanted. Satan had promised notoriety, and Sellers had gotten exactly that. But it was certainly not the kind of notoriety he had expected; what he thought he wanted was not really what he wanted at all.

Just a few words more need to be said on the whole subject of God's forgiveness. While God forgives completely, there are always ramifications when we get what we think we want.

Sean Sellers, for example, was executed by lethal injection at 12:17 a.m. on February 5, 1999 for the murders he had committed.

And King David? The first of the King's sorrows was that his son, born to Bathsheba, lived only seven days.

And several years later, one of King David's sons raped one of his daughters. And, another of David's sons, in turn, killed the rapist. Out of control sexual lust and murder. I wonder where David's children learned how to rape and murder?

I cannot say strongly enough that life is abundantly better when we get what God wants for us in the first place. But when we do make the mistake of getting what we want when we want it, instead of what God wants for us, God's unfailing love is always available to us.

By the way, the romance between Steve and I didn't work out in the end, leaving me with a broken heart. But a couple of years later, I heard that Steve had been sentenced to several years in the penitentiary for embezzling funds from his place of employment. I guess his foray into my wallet had escalated quite a bit over the years. Let's just say, at the least, my life would have been much different had I gotten what I thought I wanted.

Chapter

WHEN I'VE MESSED UP BIG TIME

8

11 Samuel 15 - Psalm 3

I t's not always an easy thing to be a preacher's kid. While the entire pastoral family lives in a glass house, the children are always under the microscope. And, from the kid's point of view, you feel as if you're in church every time the door is open. If it's a small church that your dad is pastoring, even when the door is closed you're there a lot; cleaning the bathrooms, vacuuming the carpet and mowing the lawn. This is not a bad thing, it's just a very different kind of pressure that preacher's kids experience when they're growing up.

While this pastor's daughter was growing up, our family lived in the church parsonage. Not only was the house extremely small for the four of us (my mom always said that she could stand in the middle of the living room and reach into all of the other rooms in the house), it was only separated from the church by a driveway. Members of the church who lived across the street, next door, and behind the back fence were always ready with an opinion about how their pastor's kids were behaving—and more often, how the pastors could improve their parenting skills.

Consequently, the close proximity of the church to the parsonage, the size of our house, and the fact that the church walls kept out the prying eyes of interested neighbors made the church a really tempting place to play. Even though Dad and Mom attempted to impress upon us the sanctity of the sanctuary—and frequently reminded us of the many terrible things that would happen if they caught us playing in there—my younger brother and I had a plethora of favorite things to do in the church. For example, we conducted many funerals in the church, putting to rest several of the neighbor's kids who would literally line up to play the dead body. My brother always took the role of the pastor, intoning, "Ashes to ashes, dust to dust" in his best imitation of Dad, with myself playing the double-role of organist and hysterical mourner. We also performed weddings. In fact, my first "marriage" was to Freddie Farley at the ripe old age of seven. You'd be surprised at the bouquet and wedding gown that can be made with a few wilted flowers and a drying sheet from the clothesline in the back yard.

One of my personal favorite things to do in the church though, was to fire up the old Hammond B3 organ, play absolutely dissonant chords and notes, and emulate a Boris Karloff horror movie until my little brother would run screaming out of the church, "Mommy, mommy, she's scaring me again!" The problem was that all of this playing in the church sometimes made it difficult not to play during real church time.

I remember one Sunday evening, sitting in the front row with a friend on either side of me, passing notes to one another and whispering not-so-quietly. I was suddenly surprised by the sight of my father's hand snaking down to the top of my knee and grabbing a bit of loose skin with a severe pinch. What is amazing was that Dad was preaching at the time and somehow managed to step down from the platform and deal with his errant daughter all without interrupting his sermon! So, no one but me and my wide-eyed friends were aware of the agony I was experiencing in the front row as I slid further and further down in my seat.

After finally letting go of my leg, Dad started back to the platform, but—just as my humiliation began to subside—turned around at the steps, looked directly at me, and said in an almost by-the-way tone, "I think it would be good for the children in the front row to find their parents and sit with them... Now!" I stood up and slinked back to where my mom was, sat down next to her, and thought, "Uh-oh...I'm in BIG trouble!" At that moment, I didn't worry about post-trib, pre-trib, or mid-trib doctrine; I was just praying for the Second Coming of Christ to occur before the service ended so I wouldn't have to face the music when we got home.

No such luck, however. My last great hope died when I spied from the kitchen window the last parishioner leave the sanctuary without asking for some post-church counseling. Dad locked up the church, walked across the driveway, and made his way into the house.

Without any hesitation, he grabbed my hand, led me out to what then was called the "service porch" and set me upon the washing machine so that we were at eye level. There is something about feeling guilty, knowing that you've done something so wrong that you can't look your dad in the eye even when he asks you to.

"Honey, look at Daddy."

It wasn't just that I had been a bad little girl. I had embarrassed my Dad in front of his congregation, and I recognized this.

"Honey, I said look at Daddy."

With my chin still down on my chest, my lower lip began quivering and my eyes filled with tears. It was then I felt my Dad's big hands wrap around my cheeks, and gently lift my face up so that my eyes looked into his. To my great astonishment, I did not see anger in his eyes, but rather great love for me. He told me that he was disappointed in me because he knew I was a better girl than my actions had displayed in church. Of course, disappointing my father was worse than any kind of punishment, and without even thinking I fell into his arms and began to cry out, "I'm so sorry, Daddy...I'm so sorry."

Humans really are very good a messing things up. I'm not necessarily talking about obvious sinful activity in this chapter, but rather situations that we get ourselves into because of bad decisions we make and responsibility we don't take when we should. Or even unwillingness to face the fact of our indiscretions. I'm talking about those kinds of situations where we can't necessarily say, "Wow, that was really sinful," but can say, "Oh man, I really blew it."

When we take a close look at King David's life we, of course, see him committing obvious sins. But, it may surprise you to discover that a real problem area for King David was in his parenting skills—or better yet, his lack of parenting skills. It was in his own home, that King David made some huge blunders that ended up having horrible ramifications on himself and his family. Even worse, his actions wreaked havoc on the entire nation of Israel, causing innocent people to suffer greatly.

King David had a number of children, and one of those was a son named Absalom. Absalom must have been quite the specimen of a man! Scripture says of him that there was not a man in the Kingdom of Israel any more handsome than he. In fact, "from the top of his head to the sole of his foot there was no blemish in him" (2 Samuel 14:25). What a man!

Absalom came into the scriptural picture just one chapter after David's sins of adultery and murder had been revealed publicly in open court. The circumstances surrounding Absalom's introduction are equally as heinous as the previous chapter, proving that the apple didn't fall far from the tree.

By this time in King David's life, he had several wives and many more concubines. While all the children of wives and concubines were more or less raised together, there was a strong tie between siblings born of the same mother and greater prestige given to the children of David's wives over those of his concubines. All of this to say that Absalom had a sister named Tamar whom he evidently loved very much. The mother of Absalom and Tamar was Maacah, a Geshurite princess whom King David may have married as part of a diplomatic agreement with Talmai, the Geshurite King. Because she bore the same genes as her brother, Tamar must have been a real beauty. So, it was no surprise when another one of the King's sons became attracted to her.

This son so attracted to Tamar was Amnon, the son of David's first wife, Ahinoam. Amnon was important not merely because he was the son of one of King David's wives, but also because he was the King's first-born son—and as such, the first in line for the succession to the throne.

It wasn't too long before Amnon's attraction to Tamar began to turn into something ugly. Simply said, Amnon allowed lust for her to take root in his heart. This lust became so strong that he became physically ill from his insane desire for Tamar. So, he formed a rather simple plan in order to get his great lust fulfilled.

One day, Amnon went to bed and pretended to be horribly ill. When King David went to see how he was doing he told the king, "I would really like my sister Tamar to come and give me something to eat. Send her here so she can make some of her special bread while I watch her. Then she can feed me from her own hand." Thinking absolutely nothing was amiss, the King sent word to the palace where Tamar lived—under the protection of the king, I might add—and asked her to make her way to her brother's house in order to prepare some food for him.

So, by the King's order, Tamar went to Amnon's house, kneaded the bread dough and baked it, all within Amnon's sight. When the bread was ready Tamar took the pan and tried to serve him the bread, yet he refused to eat it. "Send everyone out of here," Amnon said, and all the servants left. He turned to Tamar and said, "Bring the food in here to my bedroom so I can lie down while I eat the bread from your hand." When Tamar walked into the bedroom, however, Amnon grabbed her and said, "Lay with me, my sister!"

"No, brother," she cried. "Don't force me to do this! This kind of thing should not be happening in God's Kingdom of Israel! It will turn you into an evil and foolish man! And what about me? I'm a virgin! This will disgrace me before all of Israel!"

But Amnon wouldn't listen to her, and since he was much stronger than Tamar, he raped her. Now, this is interesting: scripture says that after the act was completed "Amnon hated her with an intense hatred. In fact, he hated her more than he had loved her" (2 Samuel 13:15). A perfect picture of self-hatred being turned outward, isn't it?

"Get up and get out!" Amnon screamed at Tamar. When she hesitated, pleading for him not to throw her out, Amnon called for a servant. "Get rid of this *thing*; get her out of my sight! And lock the door after her!" Thing? Yes, according to the Hebrew Bible, that is actually the wording he used! So the servant threw Tamar out of the house and locked the door behind her.

Well, Tamar was wearing a special gown at the time: the kind of gown virgin princesses wore to signify their status until marriage. But, with her virginity ripped away from her, Tamar took hold of her "virgin" dress, ripped it and poured ashes on her head and walked away from Amnon's house weeping aloud for what had been done to her.

When Absalom saw her, he knew exactly what had happened. "Has Amnon, your brother, had his way with you?" he asked. The question was, of course, answered in the affirmative. Absalom had two reactions to the dirty deed. The first was his sudden inclination to move Tamar into his own house. Obviously, Absalom didn't think his father, King David, had done a very good job of protecting her. So, into Absalom's house Tamar went. Second, while Absalom said not one word to Amnon about the rape, scripture says that he began to hate Amnon. You get the idea that from that very moment, he began to coldly calculate how best to avenge his sister.

When King David found out about the rape, scripture says, "He was furious" (2 Samuel 13:21). That's it? Yep. End of story. In fact, two whole years pass. And during all of that time, the King did nothing about the situation. There is absolutely no record in scripture that any disciplinary action whatever was meted out to Amnon; no record of King David consoling or comforting his daughter, Tamar. Absalom's hot anger and desire for revenge must have at least been noted by David. But, it seems King David simply ignored the entire situation.

Finally, just as Amnon felt that he'd gotten away with his assault, Absalom murdered him and fled from the King's household to live in safety with his Grandfather. So now, there was a raped daughter, a son who was suddenly and brutally murdered, and a son who was a murderer on the loose.

Another three years passed. Still, King David did absolutely nothing about the situation. How could this be? Maybe because David himself was a violator and a murderer and his own guilt hindered him from meting out discipline to his children. His earlier mistakes were bearing bitter fruit!

After the passing of time, however, King David began to miss his favorite son and decided to call him back to Jerusalem. It was only at this point, five years after the rape, that we get any indication at all that David was even a little bit willing to take action. This was David's big stab at really being a parent: the king asked Absalom to return to the palace, but then he refused to see him. Talk about putting a big exclamation point on David's lack of ability to really deal with this situation! This was parenting by default!

Another year passed.

Finally, Absalom got into the throne room to see the king. He bowed at his father's feet, and received the kiss of welcome. The end of the story? Everyone lived happily ever after? No way! That spirit of revenge— once practiced on Amnon, and totally unchecked by King David—had found a deep place in Absalom's heart. "After all," Absalom must have thought, "shouldn't it have been Amnon who was punished? Why should I suffer the king's displeasure for doing something the king should have done himself?" His rage must have festered like a boil during those six long years. Only this time it was his father, King David, who was the target. And did Absalom ever have a plan!

Absalom was not only handsome he was one smart and politically savvy young man. He would get up early in the morning and hitch horses to his chariot, so that he, and fifty paid runners going before him, could take up their place at the Judgment Gate in Jerusalem. In this manner, when anyone would come to the king with a legal problem that needed the king's judgment, Absalom would initiate a conversation with the person, suggesting that he himself be the judge. After all, he was certainly more available to the people than their king was. Absalom would then take hold of the man and kiss him as if best of friends. Wow, what a great politician! Scripture says, "In this manner Absalom dealt with all Israel who came to the king for judgment; so Absalom stole away the hearts of the men of Israel" (2 Samuel 15:6).

It took four years for Absalom to turn the hearts of the people away from King David. When he finally felt that he had captured the loyalty of the people, he told his father that he would return to Hebron, his hometown, to worship the Lord. Under this guise of worshipping the Lord, Absalom took two hundred of Israel's government leaders with him. Absalom even sent for one of King David's counselors to meet him in Hebron. And the ploy really worked! Scripture records Absalom's actions.

> *Absalom sent secret messengers throughout the tribes of Israel to say, "As soon as you hear the sound of the trumpets, then say, 'Absalom is king in Hebron.'...and so the conspiracy gained strength, and Absalom's following kept on increasing* (2 Samuel 15:12).

With this unanimous proclamation, Absalom was about to take the throne from his father. King David, his household, and his Mighty Men literally had to flee the city of Jerusalem, running for their lives. So back to the desert, where he had spent so many years running from King Saul, goes David, the anointed King—this time hiding from his own son.

I suppose one of the downsides to being King is that when you mess things up, it becomes public really quickly. It seems all of Israel was aware that King David had to flee from Jerusalem.

When on their way to the safety of the desert, a man named Shimei came out of his house cursing at King David and throwing stones at him saying, "Get out, you man of bloodshed, you scoundrel. The Lord has repaid you for all the blood you shed...You have come to ruin because you are a man of blood!" The King and all of his people continued along the journey while Shimei traveled along the hillside opposite King David, repeatedly cursing, throwing stones, and showering them with dirt. Nothing like kicking a man when he's already down! With Shimei's words ringing in their ears, King David and his Mighty Men eventually found themselves in a familiar state: hiding in a cave, fearing for their lives.

This was déjà vu all over again! I can just see the King meandering to the back of the cave, all alone, heartsick, embarrassed and hurt, falling face-down on the ground before his God. In a time of such personal and professional failure, this is what he said in Psalm 3:1-2:

> *O Lord, how many are my foes!*
> *How many rise up against me!*
> *Many are saying of me,*
> *"God will not deliver him."*

Interestingly, a Jewish *midrashim* or commentary on this Psalm calls attention to the phrase, "Many are saying of me/'God will not deliver him.'"

The commentator observes: "They were saying of David: "[How] can there be salvation for a man who had taken the lamb captive and slew the shepherd [referring to David's affair with Bathsheba and the murder of Uriah]... (William G. Braude, translator, 1987)." These historical commentators link King David's adulterous and murderous actions directly to Absalom's betrayal! At that moment, once again hiding in a cave and fearing for his life, he realized that his own past actions had radically affected his present circumstances.

So King David addressed his prayer to "O Lord" or more literally, "O *Yahweh*"—*a* particular name for God that was used for the very first time in the Book of Exodus when Moses stood before the burning bush, talking with God. He knew that the success of his mission to free the people of Israel from slavery in Egypt depended upon the power of the One who was sending him.

"Suppose I go to the Israelites and say to them, 'The God of your fathers has sent me to you,' and they ask me, 'What is his name?' asked Moses. 'Then what shall I tell them?' God replied to Moses, 'I AM WHO I AM'" (Exodus 3:14). *Yahweh.*

In addressing God as *Yahweh* David recalled the God of Israel, the God of the covenant, the God who is loyal to rescue his people—even when they really mess up. In this, God is quite different from the "many" who opposed the King. Verse 3 of Psalm 3 begins with two wonderful words: "But you."

> *But you are a shield around me, O Lord;*
> *You bestow glory on me and lift up my head.*

In contrast to all of those around him, King David addressed God with an emphatic and contrastive use of the pronoun "you." How different is God from "the many!" Rather than being a God who laid accusations and recriminations at David's door, God was a "shield around" him.

The Hebrew word that King David used for shield was *magen.* The word certainly does describe a common type of round shield that both foot soldiers and officers would carry into battle, the kind of shield that David would have been very familiar with during his days of leading the armies of Israel. But the word *magen* can also be used to describe a symbolic shield, someone who is known as a "suzerain"—a ruler who is both a protector of and a benefactor to his nation. Clearly, King David understood that although the kingship was forcibly removed from him by his son, he was still protected by God's kingship. With the metaphor "shield," David placed himself under the **protection** of the High King, who has promised to protect His own.

And, God was not only David's protector, but his benefactor as well. God gave to King David an element of His own person that is usually reserved for God alone. God was David's "glory." The simple definition of "glory" (or *kabod* in Hebrew), is "heaviness" or even better, "weightiness." Remember with me that David had just lost his kingdom, and with it the glory that goes along with being the king. Receiving "glory" from God was huge for David!

This word, "glory," is used two ways in scripture: in a literal sense and in a figurative sense.

As for "glory" in the literal sense, the term occurs in I Samuel 4:18 in which the prophet Eli is described as "heavy" or "fat." *Kabod* is used again in II Samuel 14:26 to describe Absalom's hair as being "heavy," which it truly was—scripture says that when Absalom cut his hair once a year, it weighed as much as two pounds!

The second major use of "glory" is figurative. In this case, the idea of weightiness relates to being noteworthy or impressive. Common translations we find in scripture for the word *kabod* are words like "honorable," "honored," "glorious," or "glorified."

It is important to understand that the reputation of an individual is of central importance in these usages of "glory." Certainly, a person of high social position and accompanying wealth is automatically an honored, or weighty, person in the society. But wealth itself doesn't give an individual honor. During King David's time in history, it was believed that having riches and enjoying a long life were the just rewards of a righteous life. That is, the wealthy person was honored (or weighty) not because he was rich, but because he lived the kind of righteous life that produced the wealth. In fact, scripture makes it clear that possessing the trappings of glory, riches and position without the accompanying righteousness (weightiness) of character is an offense to life itself. In God's view, a righteous, weighty character is everything.

Let's face it: at this point in David's life, he was feeling anything but righteous, anything but significant. He had lost his wealth, his position, his reputation.

Have you ever been there? Like King David, allowing echoes of your own past to cause a lack of good discipline with your children? Or have you done something really stupid—made a bad decision—becoming fodder for those who have found out about it? You may have even heard a few people say, "Well, good enough for you! You play, you pay! You made your bed, now sleep in it! It's about time you paid the piper! Even God won't get you out of this one!"

You may even feel worse about it than anyone, thinking that you've gone too far this time; thinking you really may be outside of God's graceful acts of understanding and forgiveness. After all, you've embarrassed yourself, your family, and tarnished the reputation of your God. And, you feel that you deserve what you get—that and more.

But remember what loser-of-his-kingdom-David did when he was exactly in this kind of situation? According to Psalm 3:3, he turned to his God and cried, "Oh God, YOU, in contrast to all others who mock me, hate me, desire revenge upon me, YOU protect me! YOU give me significance! YOU impart righteousness to me! **YOU lift up my head!**"

What an amazing thing! In the midst of your own shame and sense of failure, your Heavenly Father, *Yahweh,* desires to take His big hands, put them around your cheeks and lift your head so that you can see Him eye-to-eye. And trust me, what you will see there will not be anger, nor desire for retribution, but something quite unexpected. Father God will look at you straight in the eye and with great love and compassion say, "Son, Daughter, Daddy loves you."

WHEN A FRIEND BETRAYS ME

2 Samuel 15-17 / Psalm 55

N o one was more thrilled than I when Disney chose to turn C.S. Lewis' The Chronicles of Narnia: The Lion, the Witch, and the Wardrobe into a movie. For several years running, I have read the entire seven-book set of Chronicles once each year, and knowing that Hollywood would make Lewis accessible to an audience who had never read his work was exciting.

The Lion, the Witch, and the Wardrobe, Lewis' second book in the series, is about four children, Peter, Susan, Edmund and Lucy, who were sent to a professor's country home for protection from the London bombings during World War II. There, in an upstairs bedroom, they found a magical wardrobe which when entered, lead to a mystical land called Narnia. During this time in Narnia's history, the evil White Witch held the country under her wicked spell, so that in Narnia it was always winter, but never Christmas. In order to break the witch's spell, the children were to join forces with Aslan, the true Lord of Narnia, and fight the White Witch and her army.

One day, Edmund, one of the four children, made a foray into Narnia all by himself. He was quickly met on the road by a sleigh occupied by the White Witch herself. Knowing through a prophecy that the children were coming into Narnia in order to overthrow her, it was of utmost importance to the White Witch that the four children be captured before they joined up with Aslan. So, she welcomed Edmund into her sleigh and plied him with hot chocolate and Turkish Delight, magically made, telling Edmund that he could be a king in her kingdom if only he would bring his brother and sisters to her castle. Loving the idea of becoming a king more than he loved the idea of doing what was right, Edmund began to plot how he might betray his brother and sisters to the Witch.

Edmund failed miserably, showing up at the castle empty-handed. So, unable to bring Peter, Susan and Lucy into her net, the Witch was required to change her tactics. The prophecy had said that all four of the children were needed for absolute rule in Narnia. If the Witch couldn't get all four in order to secure her rule, without Edmund, neither could Aslan rule absolutely.

So, the Witch marched the bound and humiliated Edmund into Aslan's camp. She stood before Aslan, demanding Edmund's blood.

"You have a traitor in your midst," she declared.

"His offense is not against you," Aslan roared.

"Have you forgotten the laws upon which Narnia was built?" asked the witch.

Aslan growled and answered, "Don't cite the deep magic to me, witch. I was there when it was written."

"Then you'll remember well that every traitor belongs to me. His blood is my property," said the witch.

Edmund's brother, Peter, drew his sword. "Try and take him, then."

"Do you really think," laughed the witch, "that mere force will deny me my right, little king? Aslan knows that unless I have blood as the law demands, all of Narnia will be overturned and perish in fire and water. That boy will die upon the stone table—as is tradition. You dare not refuse me."

"Enough," declared Aslan. "I shall talk with you alone."

Aslan entered his tent, followed by the witch. After a short time they return. Edmund and the entire Narnian army awaited the news.

"She has renounced her claim on the son of Adam's blood," Aslan declared.

As the people begin to rejoice, the witch asked Aslan, "How can I know your promise will be kept?"

His response was a ferocious roar.

Lucy, Edmund's sister, rejoiced and smiled at Aslan. Then suddenly, as if she realized something was amiss, her smile began to fade.

What Lucy didn't know at this moment was the cost of Edmund's freedom. For it had been settled that Aslan would die on the stone table in the traitor's place.

Of course, the symbolism is clear here: Aslan is the Christ-figure dying in place of Edmund, who represents all human traitors. And even though being betrayed by someone does not always cost us our physical lives, betrayal does cause the death of our trust in someone.

King David was no stranger to betrayal. As we learned in the last chapter, his own son, Absalom, spent four years wooing the Israelites away from his father so that he could become King. Actually, Absalom's actions should not have surprised David. I have a feeling that years earlier, when number-two-son Absalom murdered number-one-son Amnon for raping Tamar, the murderous act was more about getting rid of the heir to the throne than it was about avenging the sister. If in fact Absalom coveted Israel's throne enough to kill his own half-brother for it, then David should not have been surprised that Absalom was unwilling to wait for his father's death before becoming King. I do think, however, that King David must have been greatly surprised by how easily some of his closest friends and confidants changed their allegiance to Absalom.

As we know, with Absalom's successful coup in full bloom, David ran for his life, literally on foot, from Jerusalem, along with most of his household and allies. In a short time, King David and his people were soon confronted by a rather famous hill located just outside the city: the Mount of Olives. During this time, a place of worship was situated at the top of the 2,700-foot high mountain.

So, King David and his men began to climb the hill in order to worship God. As they went, they expressed their sorrow over their loss of Jerusalem by weeping and their sense of despair by covering their heads. The King himself walked barefoot up the Mount, symbolizing the shameful exile that he was experiencing.

In the midst of King David's complete agony and humiliation, one of his men informed him, that Ahithophel had joined the conspirators with Absalom. Talk about adding sorrow on top of sorrow! You see, Ahithophel had been David's special counselor. This man had not only held one of the highest court positions possible, but was King David's confidant in most every matter. David had trusted Ahithophel above all others. He, therefore, knew how the King thought, how he fought, and virtually everything that pertained to running the Kingdom of Israel. Plus, Ahithophel's influence in Jerusalem was huge! Scripture says of him, "The counsel that Ahithophel gave in those days was treated as if God himself had spoken" (2 Samuel 16:23).

But there are a couple of things that we need to understand about Ahithophel. First, his name means "My brother is foolishness." Second, Ahithophel's son was a man named Eliam who was Bathsheba's father. On the one hand, the fact that Ahithophel was Bathsheba's grandfather could have given David a sense of profound trust in the man; after all he was David's grandfather-in-law. On the other hand, could it be that Ahithophel had simply been biding his time all along, waiting for the right moment to repay David for his adulterous act with Bathsheba and the subsequent murder of Uriah? In any case, it is clear that Ahithophel lived up to the meaning of his name in his role as a traitor to the king.

Well, for whatever reason, the fact that Ahithophel betrayed him obviously alarmed King David because he knew that whoever had the benefit of Ahithophel's advice in military or political matters would probably be successful in ruling over Israel. So David, making a word-play on Ahithophel's name, appealed to God and prayed, "O LORD, turn Ahithophel's counsel into foolishness" (2 Samuel 15:31).

As if in answer to his prayer, just as King David approached the top of the hill he was met by a man named Hushai. Hushai's clothes were ripped to shreds and he had dirt on his head in mourning for the loss of the Kingdom to Absalom. Now Hushai was known as "the Friend of David." This was not simply a description of Hushai's relationship with David, but was actually a title that described Hushai as a royal official of high standing in David's kingdom. His actual function is not described, but he could well have been another of King David's intimate counselors.

Viewing Hushai as having been sent by God, the King said to him, "Look, if you come with me you'll just be one more man among many. Instead, go back to Jerusalem and say to Absalom, 'I'm ready to be your servant, O King. I used to be your father's servant, now I'm all yours.' If you do that, Hushai, you'll be able to subvert Ahithophel's counsel for me. The priests Zadok and Abiathar, and their sons Ahimaaz and Jonathan, are already in Jerusalem. Whatever information you pick up there, give to any of those men and they will get the word to me." So, in one fell swoop, King

David was able to undermine Ahithophel's scheme and set up a spy network in Absalom's new reign. Following David's orders, Hushai made his way back to Jerusalem, arriving at the same time Absalom was entering the city.

A few days later, Hushai approached Absalom saying, "Long live the King! Long live the King!" Hushai's proclamation was obviously a bit premature, but probably worked to stroke Absalom's ego.

"Is this the way you show devotion to your good friend David? Why didn't you go with him?" asked Absalom.

"Listen," Hushai replied, "I am staying right here with the man that both God and the people have chosen to be their king. Besides, who is there other than the son left to serve? Just as I served your father, I am now ready to serve you." And with that, Hushai was welcomed into Absalom's household.

Meanwhile, as King David was making his way back down the mount, he was met with two interesting circumstances that illustrated the emotional roller coaster he was experiencing.

First, a man named Ziba met David with a string of pack animals loaded down with a hundred loaves of bread, a hundred raisin cakes, a hundred baskets of fresh fruit and a skin of wine. Much like Abigail made up for her husband Nabal's foolish actions, so Ziba did in response to Absalom's foolish deeds. This, of course, must have reminded King David that just like God took care of him and his men by the hand of Abigail many years before, God would provide for them now.

The second encounter David had was not quite so pleasant, however. As I mentioned in the last chapter, when David and his followers reached a city called Bahurim, a man named Shimei began to throw rocks and curse David. "Get lost, get lost, you butcher," Shimei screamed, "God has finally paid you back for all the blood you shed in Saul's household when you stole his kingdom. God has now given the Kingdom to your son Absalom. Look at you now! You're ruined!"

When one of King David's men wanted to kill Shimei, David told him that in comparison to what his own son had done to him, Shimei's curses were nothing. "Besides," the King said, "maybe the Lord will see my distress and repay me with good for the cursing I am receiving for Him." For quite a ways down the road, Shimei continued to throw stones and dirt and curse at David.

Scripture then says, "By the time they reached the Jordan River, David and all the people with him were exhausted. There they rested and were revived" (2 Samuel 16:13).

It is thought that King David wrote Psalm 55 during this particular time in his life.

> *Listen to my prayer, O God, do not ignore my plea; hear me and answer me.*
> *My thoughts trouble me and I am distraught at the voice of the enemy, at the stares of the wicked; for they bring down suffering upon me and revile me in their anger.*
>
> *My heart is in anguish within me; the terrors of death assail me. Fear and trembling have beset me; horror has overwhelmed me. I said, "Oh, that I had the wings of a dove! I would fly away and be at rest—I would flee far away and stay in the desert;*
> *Selah*
> *I would hurry to my place of shelter, far from the tempest and storm."*

Confuse the wicked, O Lord, confound their speech, for I see violence and strife in the city. Day and night they prowl about on its walls; malice and abuse are within it. Destructive forces are at work in the city; threats and lies never leave its streets.

If an enemy were insulting me, I could endure it; if a foe were raising himself against me, I could hide from him. But it is you, a man like myself, my companion, my close friend, with whom I once enjoyed sweet fellowship as we walked with the throng at the house of God.

Let death take my enemies by surprise; let them go down alive to the grave, for evil finds lodging among them.

But I call to God, and the LORD saves me. Evening, morning and noon I cry out in distress, and he hears my voice. He ransoms me unharmed from the battle waged against me, even though many oppose me. God, who is enthroned forever, will hear them and afflict them—
Selah
men who never change their ways and have no fear of God.

My companion attacks his friends; he violates his covenant. His speech is smooth as butter, yet war is in his heart; his words are more soothing than oil, yet they are drawn swords.

Cast your cares on the LORD and he will sustain you; he will never let the righteous fall. But you, O God, will bring down the wicked into the pit of corruption; bloodthirsty and deceitful men will not live out half their days.

But as for me, I trust in you.

Look at how David described his situation: he was troubled, distraught, feeling terrified—fear and trembling and horror had nearly overwhelmed him. All of these things indicate the inward disposition of a man who was facing yet one more war. And this time the battle would be fought not with a historic enemy of Israel, but with fellow Israelites led by his own son. This was almost more than David could bear! *The Message* renders David's words in this way:

> *This isn't the neighborhood bully mocking me—*
> *I could take that.*
> *This isn't a foreign devil spitting invective—*
> *I could tune that out.*
> *It's you! My best friend!*
> *Those long hours of leisure as we walked arm in arm,*
> *God a third party to our conversation...*

While David didn't name Ahithophel specifically in this Psalm, it is very possible that this was the man to whom David was referring. Note that David did not moan and groan about the loss of his kingdom, nor did he display surprise about his son's behavior. What really hurt David was the betrayal of his friend. And, not only did Ahithophel betray him, he was actively involved in using all of his wisdom and knowledge to kill David and his followers.

This was a tough place for David. He was not only outmanned, he was out-counseled. The war could well be won on the basis of Ahithophel's advice alone. Look at how David prayed: "Confuse the wicked, O Lord, and confound their speech." The battle David was waging in prayer was not one fought with spears and swords; brilliantly, David asked God to take Ahithophel's greatest talent and make it invalid in the enemy's deliberations. And did God ever answer David's prayer!

It wasn't long after Hushai's entrance into Jerusalem that Absalom called a war counsel together. "Let me handpick 12,000 men," Ahithophel offered, "and we'll go after David tonight. We'll come down on him while he and his men are exhausted and we'll take them by surprise. We'll kill David while the rest of his army runs in terror. Then, we'll bring the rest of the people back to you unharmed."

Well, the rest of the elders with him thought this was an excellent idea, but Absalom said, "Let's get a second opinion on this—call in Hushai and let's hear what he has to say."

When Hushai heard about the plan he said, "This is not a bad plan, but you know that David and his men are brave and experienced fighters. On top of that, they're all probably as mad as a she-bear robbed of her cubs. I doubt very seriously that you'll find them napping at a time like this. I'll just bet he's holed up in some cave somewhere planning for your attack. If he is successful in ambushing you Absalom, word will get back that he slaughtered your army. Even if your men are valiant with hearts like lions, they would melt with fear because everyone knows what a warrior your father is and that all of those with him are really brave."

"So," Hushai continued, "this is what I advise: Gather all of Israel's men, from Dan to Beersheba—as many as the sand on the seashore—and you, Absalom, lead them into battle. Then we'll attack David wherever he is, and we'll fall on him like the dew falls on the earth. And give no quarter! We'll kill him and all of his people. If he withdraws into a city, we'll bring ropes and drag the very walls down until not even a brick will be left standing!"

With this rousing speech, Absalom and all of his company agreed that Hushai's counsel was better than the counsel of Ahithophel. Almost parenthetically, scripture adds, "God had determined to discredit the counsel of Ahithophel so as to bring ruin on Absalom." Just as David had prayed in Psalm 55, God performed!

In order to fulfill his promise to David, Hushai immediately informed the priests Zadok and Abiathar what had happened in Absalom's war council. Then he said, "Tell David not to spend the night this side of the river; cross it immediately or the king and everyone with him will be swallowed up." So, the priests gave the message to their sons Jonathan and Ahimaaz who (after hiding in a well from Absalom's men) finally got word to David of all that had occurred.

Obviously, God was not unaware of the situation in which King David found himself. In the midst of one of the worse times in King David's life, he turns to his God, the One who would never betray him. Even more, Psalm 55 tells us that the King was assured that God would perform four specific acts on his behalf. So, not only did the King rejoice in the fact that God had actually confused the wicked and confounded their speech, just has he had prayed, David also knew that while he was biding his time in the desert, 1) God would hear his voice when he cried out (verse 17); 2) God would save him (verse16); 3) God would ransom him (verse 18); and that, 4) God would sustain him (verse 22). Let's take a closer look at the things God does for the loser-of-his-kingdom-and-friends, King David.

David declared that when he cried out in distress, God would hear his voice. In the Old Testament, hearing was never passive. Effective hearing always involved the idea of both understanding what was said and responding to what was said. The amazing thing here is that this kind of hearing is usually descriptive of a Sovereign to a subject. It is picture of one of the King's servants saying in response to the King's command, "To hear is to obey." This is a word that describes hearing-in-action.

When David asserts that God will hear him, however, this is not David commanding God to hear and obey. Rather, scripture says that David cried out to God in distress. It is this "crying out" for help that secures the fact that God Himself is involved in working on King David's behalf. No wonder King David did not simply cry in his distress, but rather cried out to God; he knew that God would understand and respond to him in his distress. What an amazing capacity God has to perform His wondrous works! Look at the ways in which God responds to the King's cry:

David declares that the God who hears will "save" him. The word "save" here in Psalm 55:16 is the Hebrew word *yāša*. This is a really common word that is used 353 times in the Old Testament. The word itself may be commonly used, but the meaning of the word is anything but common.

A root meaning of *yāša*, "save," is to "make wide" or "make sufficient"; this root is in contrast to the word *sārar*, or "narrow," taking on the meaning to "be restricted" or to "cause distress." So, that which is wide (*yāša*), connotes freedom from distress and the ability to pursue one's own objectives. However, to move from distress to safety requires deliverance. In the Old Testament, this deliverance must come from somewhere outside the person who was oppressed, since the oppressed person was too weak to deliver himself. The one who brings deliverance is known as the "savior." For David, it was *Yahweh* who fashioned the deliverance, the One who is his Savior. God would save David out of his "narrow place" and set him in a "wide place" where once again King David would be able to function as King of all Israel.

David then knew that God would not only save him, but ransom him, as well. Psalm 55:17 says, "He ransoms me unharmed from the battle waged against me, even though many oppose me." The basic meaning of "ransom" is to achieve the transfer of ownership from one to another through payment of a price or an equivalent substitute. It is also used to speak of the redemption of a man's life who is under the sentence of death. But more importantly here, the word is also used to describe a warrior who fights the battle on behalf of those in his kingdom, in effect, ransoming the kingdom from the enemy through the giving of his life in battle. Remember with me that David knew that if he had any hope of being restored to his throne, there would be war. But King David was assured that God would fight the battle for him, ransoming the Kingdom of Israel back to its rightful King.

Last, King David was also aware that God would sustain him. This is the Hebrew word *kûl*. The primary meaning of this root is "to contain as does a vessel." It occurs thirty-eight times in the Old Testament. About half of those times, *kûl* describes how much a certain vessel can hold. The other nineteen occurrences, however, show the particularized meaning "to provide with food," and not just a little bit of food. The word "sustain" in this verse describes a vessel that is absolutely filled to the brim.

Did God answer King David's prayer?

Well, look at how this circumstance in King David's life played out. He did cross the Jordan with all of his people, just as Hushai had advised him to do. When David reached the city of Mahanaim, three men came out to meet him: Shobi ("the glorious one") son of Nahash, Makir, the son of the great chief Ammiel of Lodebar, and Barzillai ("the iron man") of Rogelim. These were all men of great notoriety in the city of Mahanaim who not only brought their swords and their pledge of loyalty to the king's cause, but also brought with them immediate necessities for all the people. They provided bedding, bowls and articles of pottery, and foodstuff— wheat, barley, flour, grain, beans and lentils, honey and cheese, and sheep—for King David and his people to eat.

God **really did** hear King David's voice in the midst of his great betrayal.

Have you had a friend or family member, maybe even a coworker, who has sold you out? Someone who has betrayed you in order to save themselves? I sure have. And I suppose the most frustrating thing is that there was not a thing I could say or do to repair the damage my turncoat friend had caused.

That's why David gives us this remedy at the end of Psalm 55. He says, "Cast your cares on the LORD and he will sustain you; he will never let the righteous fall."

It should be blatantly obvious to us that according to Psalm 55, only the Lord can fix this kind of circumstance. Just as God had worked to discredit Ahithophel's advice so that David's life would be saved, only God can do the work necessary to repair the damage a betrayer causes. There is, however, an act that we must do that precedes God's acts of hearing our cry, save us, ransom us and sustain us. David says that we must, "Cast," or better, "Hurl away" our cares. Because this word is in the imperative tense here, the act of "hurling away" our cares is not a suggestion, it is a command! We are not to hold on to the heavy burden of the pain of our betrayal but rather throw all that pain upon the Lord.

Interestingly, Psalm 55 not only describes David's experience with his traitor-friend but is also viewed by biblical scholars as one of David's Messianic Psalms because it is such a strong reflection of Jesus' experience of betrayal by Judas.

Look at the parallels between David's experience and Jesus' experience in the story. All the utterly real issues swirling around David, Absalom, the Israelites and God, also swirled around Jesus as He moved toward the cross. One must think that the Gospel writers were acutely aware of this; they depicted Jesus' Maundy Thursday walk to the Mount of Olives in ways graphically reminiscent of David's agonizing journey up the very same mountain. Especially the details of Judas' betrayal of Jesus, have a remarkable similarity to Ahithophel's betrayal of the Lord's anointed, King David.

How in the world did Jesus make it through the agonizing journey to the cross, suffering Judas' betrayal all along the way?

A man who saw first-hand the last few days of Jesus' life, the Apostle Peter, said that Jesus endured the suffering by "entrust[ing] himself to He who judges justly." Jesus Himself hurled all of the pain of His betrayal upon the Father who had the ability to bring justice in the end. Jesus knows what it feels like to be betrayed!

Let me talk just a little bit here about this whole idea of casting our cares upon the Lord. The Hebrew word for "cares" used here is *yehab*. This word is translated two ways in the Old Testament. It is, of course, the word for "burden" just as we see here in Psalm 55. But it is also the word for, "that which is given," or even simpler, "a gift." In order to render the word correctly, the translators of the Hebrew Bible into English always allow the context of the word to guide their translation. So, sometimes we see *yahab* translated with the idea of "that which is given" as in the scripture, "Absalom said to Ahithophel, "**Give** (*yehab*) us your advice." In this case, Ahithophel's advice was actually seen as a gift given to Absalom.

O.K., I know what you're thinking. How in the world can a burden and a gift possibly be related in any way?

In 1997, Holly Payne, stopping on the road to assist two cyclists, was struck by a drunk driver and propelled several dozen feet onto her back. Suffering a broken pelvis as well as a shattered femur that required a titanium plate and ten screws to hold her leg together, Payne survived the physical agony by promising herself, "If I'm alive, I'm going to write." After nearly a year in a wheel chair, then behind a walker, on crutches, then a cane, in addition to months of intensive physical therapy, Payne was finally able to function normally. True to the promise she made to herself, Payne has since that time written several novels and has recently returned to her alma mater, USC, to teach in their Professional Writing Program. Looking back on the fifteen years since the horrible accident, she says, "In many ways, **getting struck was a gift**, and it set me on the course of a writing life."

Hmmm. A broken pelvis, a shattered leg and nine months in a wheel chair, a gift?

Sometimes, the experience of being betrayed can end up being a gift. That was certainly the case for Peter, Susan and Lucy of Narnia.

As Lucy, Susan, and Peter were running for their lives in the attempt to escape from the vicious jaws of the White Witch's wolf-minions, they found that the wolves had come so close them that the children had no choice but to scramble under a snowy overhang—the most immediately convenient place to hide. Holding their breaths and fearing for their lives, the children huddled together waiting to hear the inevitable snarl of the wolves and see the snapping of their jaws. But, as the children silently hid, they surprisingly heard a jingling sound. At first, they thought it was the White Witch come to capture them. But, as they crept out of their place of hiding in order to investigate, they were astonished to find Father Christmas standing there beside his sleigh, resplendent in his red suit. "I've come at last," he said. "The White Witch has kept me out for a long time, but I have got in at last. Aslan is on the move. The witch's magic is weakening."

Well, you can't have the appearance of Father Christmas without gifts. "And now for your presents," said Father Christmas. For Peter, there was a silver-colored shield with a red lion, as well as a sword with a gold hilt, a sheath and a sword belt. For Susan, there was a bow and a quiver full of arrows and a little ivory horn. Lucy received a glass bottle filled with a healing cordial and a dagger for self-defense.

Magically, Father Christmas pulled a large tray out of his bag containing cups and saucers and sugar and cream, and even a sizzling hot teapot. Then he cried out, "Merry Christmas! Long live the true King!" cracked his whip, and was off before anyone knew he was leaving

But, wait a minute. What about gifts for Edmund? Well, this is the point I want to make about traitorous behavior. While gifts were being given out by Father Christmas, Edmund was being held captive in the White Witch's palace. And while Edmund was ultimately restored to relationship with his siblings and with Aslan, for the entire time he was in Narnia, he was giftless.

It's possible that one the ramifications of betrayal is becoming so bound by the desire to be a king, that gifts bringing victory, help and healing to others are entirely missed. You see, there's something about betrayal that becomes so self-serving, all else and everyone else takes second place to the all-consuming "me."

In fact, when Ahithophel realized that his counsel to Absalom was not going to be followed, he went home, made out his will, put his house in order, and then did what psychologists call the most selfish of all human acts. Ahithophel, like Judas centuries later, committed suicide by hanging himself. What an end to a man whose words of influence were once equated with the very words of God!

Have you been betrayed? Has someone used you? Said horrible things about you? Betrayed a confidence that has caused you and others pain? According to King David, during these times, God Himself will hear you and respond to your distress. When life happens, God will save you and set you back on a wide path of healing and renewal and restoration. God Himself will ransom you by fighting the battle you cannot fight for yourself. And God will sustain you; He will fill you to the brim and restore to you that which you thought was lost.

And you, too, just might discover that your greatest burden has become your greatest gift.

AFTERWORD

WHEN THERE'S A BREAK IN THE ACTION

2 Samuel 22 & Psalm 18

W e've spent quite a bit of time discussing how we should work through the issues of life when they happen to us. The unexpected results of "life happening" are probably what drove someone to coin the phrase "Life is hard, and then you die." But honestly, while it seems sometimes as if our reality is filled with battle after battle after battle, there really does come a time in our lives when we are able to take a deep breath, throw our sword to the ground, and know that victory has finally been won; there is light at the end of the tunnel.

What we really want to know, deep down in our soul, is why in the world God allows horrible difficulties to touch our lives in the first place. The question has been posed in many different contexts: "How could a God of love allow this to happen?" I once heard the great theologian R.C. Sproul answer that question by posing another: "How could a God of justice and righteousness allow totally depraved humans to live at all?" Unfortunately, the answers to both of these questions will never be answered fully while we're on this side of heaven; last time I looked, humans still didn't have the ability to delve into the depths of the purposes of God. I can tell you though, that one of the big reasons why God allows us to fight battles when life happens is because of what we learn in the process.

There are two vital things we must learn as we go through the difficulties of life. First, **we'll never make it through life on our own**; and second, **it is in the hardships that we come to know God intimately**. To illustrate the first of these lessons—we are not alone—we turn to 2 Samuel 21, where there is a succinct list of four battles fought by Israel against their archenemy the Philistines:

> *Once again there was a battle between the Philistines and Israel. David went down with his men to fight against the Philistines, and he became exhausted. And Ishbi-Benob, one of the descendants of Rapha, whose bronze spearhead weighed three hundred shekels and who was armed with a new sword, said he would kill David. But Abishai son of Zeruiah came to David's rescue; he struck the Philistine down and killed him. Then David's men swore to him, saying, "Never again will you go out with us to battle, so that the lamp of Israel will not be extinguished."*

In the course of time, there was another battle with the Philistines, at Gob. At that time Sibbecai the Hushathite killed Saph, one of the descendants of Rapha.

In another battle with the Philistines at Gob, Elhanan son of Jaare-Oregim the Bethlehemite killed Goliath the Gittite, who had a spear with a shaft like a weaver's rod.

In still another battle, which took place at Gath, there was a huge man with six fingers on each hand and six toes on each foot—twenty-four in all. He also was descended from Rapha. When he taunted Israel, Jonathan son of Shimeah, David's brother, killed him. These four were descendants of Rapha in Gath, and they fell at the hands of David and his men.

The first few verses of this passage give us the reason why King David never fought with his men in battle again. Scripture says that "David became exhausted." I love the Hebrew word here for "exhausted." It's the word *uwph* and is pronounced "oof." The word even sounds like a short form of "I'm exhausted!" It actually means to "fly about" or "hover." Picture a bird that has flown so far and has batted its wings so long that it's absolutely worn out. We get the idea that David had flailed at the enemy with his sword for so long that his arms felt like lead; he could hardly pick up his own weapon any longer.

But just when the King was about to lose his life, his nephew Abishai rescued him. Abishai stepped in and killed Ishbi-Benob. From this battle on, David's men fought on his behalf lest "the lamp of Israel" be snuffed out. In the second battle, it was Sibbecai, one of David's Thirty Might Men, who killed Saph, the Philistine; in the third battle, Jaare-Oregim killed another Philistine named Goliath; and finally, in the fourth,

Jonathan, another of David's nephews, killed the six-fingered, six-toed Philistine giant in Goliath's hometown.

So while it's a given that we can't live life successfully without God beside us, it is also true that he has given us friends to help us negotiate the difficulties of life. Just as King David learned when life happened to him, we also need companions when life happens to us.

Journalist and author Bob Greene told the following story in his book *And You Know You Should Be Glad: A True Story of Lifelong Friendship*:

> There are a handful of people, during your lifetime, who know you well enough to understand when the right thing to say is to say nothing at all. Those people—and there will be, at most, only a few of them— will be with you during your very worst times....
>
> When, during an already painful juncture in my life, my wife died. I was so numb that I felt dead myself. In the hours after her death, as our children and I tried in vain to figure out what to do next, how to get from hour to hour, the phone must have been ringing, but I have no recollection of it.
>
> The next morning—one of those mornings when you awaken, blink to start the day, and then, a dispiriting second later, realize anew what has just happened and feel the boulder press you against the earth with such weight that you fear you will never be able to get up—the phone rang, and it was Jack.
>
> I didn't want to hear any voice—even his voice. I just wanted to cover myself with darkness. I knew he would be asking if there was anything he could do. But I should have known that he'd already done it.
>
> "I'm in Chicago," he said. I misunderstood him; I thought he was offering to come to Chicago.
>
> "I took the first flight this morning," he said. He had heard; he had flown in. "I know you probably don't want to see anyone," he said. "That's all right. I've checked into a hotel, and I'll just sit in the room in case you need me

to do anything. I can do whatever you want, or I can do nothing.

"He meant it. He knew the best thing he could do was to be present in the same town; to tell me he was there. And he did just sit there—I assume he watched TV, or did some work, but he waited until I gathered the strength to say I needed him. He helped me with things no man ever wants to need help with; mostly he sat with me and knew I did not require conversation, did not welcome chatter, did not need anything beyond the knowledge he was there. He brought food for my children and, by sharing my silence; he got me through those days (Greene, 2006).

Let's take a look at the second vital thing we learn when life happens.

I love what scripture says in 2 Samuel 22:1: "David sang to the Lord the words of this song **when the Lord delivered him from the hand of all his enemies** and from the hand of Saul." This indicates a huge "Whew!" moment for King David. After years of running and fighting and fighting some more, David was at that moment experiencing a break in the action.

I seriously doubt that he hopped on a plane and went to Maui for some well-deserved rest, but the King did take time somewhere to reflect on his life. And David being David, what we have as a result, are his thoughts written in a lyrical form. This particular song of David is recorded for us in two places in scripture, with only a few minor differences: 2 Samuel 22:2-51 and Psalm 18. While all scripture is vitally important, I have discovered that when things are repeated twice, this is something we really need to pay attention to! So take a look at what King David had to say when the battles had been won according to Psalm 18:

I love you, O LORD, my strength.

The LORD is my rock, my fortress and my deliverer; my God is my rock, in whom I take refuge. He is my shield and the horn of my salvation, my stronghold.

I call to the LORD, who is worthy of praise, and I am saved from my enemies.

Although David's song is a full 51 verses long, the only real notable difference between Psalm 18 **and** 2 Samuel 22 is the way in which Psalm 18 begins; for whatever reason, the first verse of Psalm 18 is not included in 2 Samuel, but it is very important. David said in Psalm 18:1, "I love you, Lord, my Strength." The word usually used to describe "love" in any relationship is the Hebrew word *'ahab* and it's used literally hundreds of times in the Old Testament. But noteworthy in this verse is that David chose to use an entirely different word to describe his love for the Lord. The word is *racham*. What makes the use of *racham* so unusual is that it is the word normally used for God's expression of love to humankind. The verb form of the word is associated with a mother's love and care for her children. *Racham* is a deep love that someone has for another that arises from intimate knowledge of the one who is loved.

King David made it clear as his song continues that this intimacy arose from a constant awareness of God's companionship in a series of dangerous and mortal crises. This intimate knowledge of God's nature is expressed in the first few verses of this song in two related themes. One theme is military: God was the King's "deliverer," shield," "the horn (or "strength") of my salvation, and "safe retreat." The second theme calls to mind the wilderness which for so long was part of David's life-experience;

God was David's "fortress," "stronghold" and "rock." I would dare say that King David would never have known God in this way without experiencing his years of hiding in the desert, his years of running, his years of fighting bloody battles; even his times of sinful actions and bad fathering. David came to know his God intimately—the God who delivered him and protected him and saved him.

David next asserted that the Lord is worthy of praise. So why should King David praise God after all of the difficulties he had been through? Simply because every time David was in mortal danger, he cried to the Lord for help, and He saved him from his enemies. But let me remind you that the final salvation of God sometimes took years, with many battles to be fought in the meantime. Remember, for example, that the anointed-king David was forced to run from Saul for years before he actually became King of Israel.

During WWII there was a British soldier named MacDonald who, along with a Scottish chaplain, bailed out of an airplane behind German lines. They were summarily captured and put in a prison camp, where the Americans and the British were separated by a high wire fence. For some reason, MacDonald was put in the American barracks while the Scottish chaplain was housed with the British.

Every day the two men would meet at the high wire fence and exchange a greeting. Unknown to the guards, the Americans had a little homemade radio able to get news from the outside—something more precious than food in a prison camp. Every day, MacDonald would take a headline or two to the fence and share it with the chaplain in the ancient Gaelic language, which was indecipherable to the Germans.

One day, news came over the little radio that the German High Command had surrendered, and the war was over. MacDonald took the news to his friend, then stood and watched him disappear into the British barracks. A moment later, a roar of celebration came from those barracks.

Life in that camp was transformed. Men walked around singing and shouting, waving at the guards, even laughing at the dogs. When the German guards finally heard the news three nights later, they fled into the dark leaving the gates unlocked. The next morning, the British and Americans walked out of the prison as free men. Yet they had truly been set free three days earlier by the wonderful news of the war's end.

So, be encouraged, my friend! Even though the circumstances in which you find yourself may not yet be resolved, your cry to the Lord has been heard, and you can praise Him for the final deliverance. In the meantime, when life happens, look around you—you just might find people who are waiting to stand with you. In fact, like those in the prison camp, you may discover the good news of your victory comes through an unexpected source. Above all, allow God to lead you into a new, intimate understanding of Himself.

When life happens to you…let Him be the rock on which you stand; let Him be your shield of defense until the final victory comes!

Works Cited

Greene, B. (2006). *And You Know You Should Be Glad: A True Story of Lifelong Friendship.* New York: HarperCollins.